RIVER MUSIC

River Music

A FLY FISHER'S FOUR SEASONS

JAMES R. BABB

Illustrations by C. D. Clarke

THE LYONS PRESS
Guilford, Connecticut
An Imprint of the Globe Pequot Press

Copyright © 2001 by James R. Babb

First Lyons Press paperback edition, 2005

The Lyons Press is an imprint of The Globe Pequot Press.

10 9 8 7 6 5 4 3 2 1

Printed in the United States of America

ISBN 1-59228-712-3

The Library of Congress has previously cataloged an earlier (hardcover) edition as follows:

Babb, James R.
  River music : a fly fisher's four seasons / James R. Babb.
  p.cm.
  ISBN 1-58574-279-1 (hc)
  1. Fly fishing—Anecdotes. I. Title.
SH456 .B243 2001
799.1'24—dc21
                                    2001029901

To scribbling putationers everywhere

And this our life, exempt from public haunt,
Finds tongues in trees, books in the running brooks,
Sermons in stones, and good in everything.

—William Shakespeare, *As You Like It*

Contents

Explanations, Confessions, Excuses, and Related Preliminary Throat Clearings

> *I have not at all studied to make a book; but I have studied somewhat because I had made it, if it is studying somewhat to skim over and pinch, by his head or feet, now one author and then another, not at all in order to form my own opinions, but certainly to assist, second, and serve those long since formed.*
>
> —MICHEL EYQUEM DE MONTAIGNE,
> "Of Giving the Lie"

𝓘'm slouched in an Adirondack chair on my office porch, tiny computer balanced across my lap, coffee steaming on the armrest, a perfect springtime symphony playing in the background: the soft bassooning of a mourning dove; the flautist burble of robins; the shrill fifing of white-throated sparrows; the castanet cackle of tree frogs; the basso *burump* of bullfrogs; the washboard ratchet of green frogs; the stuttering timpani roll of a grouse calling to the neighbor's chugging John Deere; the *flip-flip-splip* of little trout chasing speckle-winged mayflies in the pond. Underpinning these soloists is a hydraulic string section endlessly gnawing away at granite, macerating fallen trees, dodging and weaving around boulders newly rearranged by the winter's ice—a string section that never stops playing and never repeats the same passage, always making music, always rewriting the score. It's the music of a river, or at least a brook, rushing along a hundred yards from my chair and my coffee, cooling now, and the little computer, its battery dying now, and the office-door phoebe, racking her little head and fiercely chakking my way.

She wants me gone, and who am I to argue? After all, I'm just piddling around on the office porch writing inconsequential tales about fish and fishing, and the phoebe is going about the serious business of raising a family, the tenth generation to issue from a nest precariously plastered above the office door. And so I head back up to the house, with its bright lights and complaining cats and endlessly whirring machinery—freezer, refrigerator, microwave, clocks, fax machines, answering machines, laser printers, hard drives, monitors: the incessant sixty-cycles-per-second symphony of harnessed electricity—a modern house built for living a modern life; for processing, storing, and preparing food; for processing, storing, and preparing words; for editing, corresponding, digesting, and excreting the endless reams of administrivia that infest the publishing business that more or less pays for it all. The house is good for all that, but it's no good for writing. For playing my small solos I need calmer surroundings and the solid underpinnings of river music.

I grew up in a house filled with music, river and otherwise. My father was a lunatic-fringe fly fisherman and a locally famous bass singer. Everywhere he went he sang, from bathtub to trout stream, practicing everything from barbershop to Bach for performances with his quartet or the church choir or the countywide choral society, always in that deep rumbling voice that underpinned the soloists. To this day I can barely recognize a tune, from "The Old Oaken Bucket" to Handel's *Messiah,* until I hear the bass line. To me, melodies are mere ear candy. I find the truth in music hiding in its underpinnings.

I was born into music, but I'm not a musician. I can carry a tune, but my adenoidal voice scratches like a fingernail on a blackboard, and I only sing to amuse myself or annoy my friends. A long time ago I was a pretty good trumpet player, but I gave it up for the guitar when I first heard Eric Clapton and the Three Kings: Albert, Freddy, and B. B. I gave up the guitar years ago when a steel cable broke while winching a truck out of a bog and pulled my steel-string-hooking thumb out of its socket. Or at least that's the story I usually tell. I actually gave up the guitar because I realized I would never be truly good at it, bum thumb or not, and that having my hand in a cast for six months was as good an excuse as any to quit before I became a sad old man playing bad blues for beers in cheap bars.

And so I became a listener and not a creator of music, and from too much listening at too much volume I became musically blessed in a different way, for I hear the music of rivers wherever I go. My doctor calls this "tinnitus" and says he can cure it, or at least diminish it. But I think of all the times the mindless mouthings of interchangeable bosses or the whine of jet engines or petulant infants yowling to one another like coyotes on the prairie have been if not drowned then at least partly submerged by a self-generated concert of crackling riffles and booming rapids, and I say, No Way: I like things the way they are. Hearing the music of rivers even when they're far away is a gift, not a disease, one that helps me do something I'm compelled to do, which is describe what I hear to people who care to listen—to try, in my own poor way, to give verbal life to the musical foundations of Life that rumble just subaudible all around us and, on bright booming trout streams, roar to the surface and electrify the soul.

These are deep feelings, strongly felt, and because I am a Modern American Male it is my duty to make fun of them. What else can I do?

When I remember that the world's population has tripled in my lifetime, I get scared. When I remember there are twice as many Americans now as when I was born, one year before the center point of the last century, I get scared. When I think of all the lonely sylvan trout streams that once sang their own songs and now retch and stew in the carpark tailwaters of metastasizing strip malls and twenty-acre ranchettes, I get scared. When I think of a world where the wild has become more novelty than norm, and fly fishing not a spiritual sojourn in the silent places but a competitive sport played out elbow to elbow on hard-pressed waters, I get scared. When I notice that every day my belt buckle and Adam's apple grow closer together and my hairline is chasing cherished memories down the back of my neck, I get scared. Who wouldn't?

"Humor," James Thurber wrote, "is emotional chaos remembered in tranquility." Because so much of fly fishing involves remembered tranquility and so much of modern life is emotional chaos, I've a bottomless well of fears to make fun of, an endless supply of the raw materials for humor. And humor, Mark Twain wrote in his autobiography, "must not professedly teach and it must not professedly preach, but it must do both if it would live forever." I entertain no hopes of living forever, but I'd like to at least float a thought balloon or two above the occasional laugh. And that's what this is all about—the occasional laugh, the occasional thought, a bit about fly fishing and a bit about Life, and all of it shored up by the music of rivers.

A few years ago, having edited several score issues of a magazine and several hundred books and feeling it was my turn in the barrel, authorially speaking, I wrote a book of my own called *Crosscurrents*. The people I wanted to like it did and the people I didn't want to like it didn't. Thus encouraged, emboldened, or deluded, I present here book the second.

As was the case with *Crosscurrents,* a good chunk of this collection came from my columns in *Gray's Sporting Journal.* Freed from the need to cater to a broad audience and from the straitjacket of a magazine column's fourteen-hundred-word length, I have rewritten these pieces in varying degrees and sometimes have taken them in quite different directions from their compressed and slightly constipated originals—the difference between the Chambers Brothers' "Time" on Top Forty and the long version on the album, the one tight and concise and the other either free-flowing and improvisational or long and self-indulgent, depending on your viewpoint.

"Little Jewels," "Nature's Call," "Those Who Say Woo," "Little Big Business," and "The Vice of the Vise" are all new to this book. A small portion of "Tales of the Vienna Sausages" appeared originally as a campfire-cooking piece written for *The Field,* which is the British equivalent of *Gray's,* only 150 years older and with more pictures of sheep and Lady Blemish enjoying her Pink coat and saddle.

My eternal gratitude goes to the usual suspects and a few new faces for their help with this book: To Ted Leeson, for liking my writing much better than I do, and for pointing out, in early drafts, where I'd hit the mark and where my carpentry was painfully visible. To my wife, Linda, who tells me when I'm being thick and when I'm being precious, who always keeps me laughing and forgives my momentary lapses of reason. To Mary Hood, whose philosophical revelations helped float me off a number of rough spots where I'd high-centered myself. To Cheryce Marie Kramer, an unrequited midlife crisis who became a chapter, and later a true friend. To Laura Jorstad, who has copyedited both my books so transparently you'd never have known she was there, unless she hadn't been. To Nick Lyons, Tony Lyons, and Jonathan McCullough at The Lyons Press, who always said the right things and displayed the patience of saints as I missed deadline after deadline. To the folks who have encouraged me to continue my life of crime—pleasant people whose names I've forgotten who came up to me at book signings and quoted passages I'd forgotten writing; a wildlife biologist named Dan Landeen who liked my first book well enough to make me a fine cane rod inscribed with CROSSCURRENTS and my name; a handful of Real Writer friends who claim to like my stuff enough to drive their friends and loved ones nuts by reading it aloud. And most important, to the people who opened their wallets and bought my first book, thus encouraging me to write another.

Thanks to the music makers who have underpinned my life, to Vivaldi and Purcell, Redding and Reed, Corelli and Copland, Marley and Mozart, Waters and Gilmour, Clapton and the Three Kings. And I mustn't forget the rivers and the brooks and the streams. Thanks to a life lived on their banks and to too much loud music, I can hear them wherever I go.

First Movement

Spring

Who says a painting must look like life?
He sees only with children's eyes.
Who says a poem must stick to the theme?
Poetry is certainly lost on him.
Who'd think one dot of red
Could call up a whole unbounded spring!

—TUNG-P'O,
Sung dynasty

1

Darling Buds of May

Rough winds do shake the darling buds of May,
And summer's lease hath all too short a date:
Sometime too hot the eye of heaven shines,
And often is his gold complexion dimm'd;
And every fair from fair sometime declines,
By chance or nature's changing course untrimm'd;

—WILLIAM SHAKESPEARE,
Sonnet XVIII

In the chronological wingshoot of a winterbound angler, I stand in one slice of time and aim toward another, looking out into winter's bleak wasteland and seeing the soft bloom of May.

Up here where I live, north of forty-four, halfway between New Hampshire and New Brunswick at the mouth of Maine's Penobscot River, winter is an interminable gauntlet of adversity—five months of forting up behind stout walls and feeding the woodstove, the body, and the soul.

In winter folks up here go crazy—woods queer, cabin fever, Seasonal Affective Disorder. SAD comes from the shortened day and dearth of sunlight, they say, and scientifically speaking that may be true. But I think sad*ness* comes more from brooding over things that were and now are not, things that could but likely won't, things that should but never will. If a Maine winter is nothing else, it is prime time for brooding over life's inherent inequities, a fertile incubator of unrealized expectations.

You'd think January would be the worst. It is, after all, the coldest month. But there's more to misery than the level of mercury in the tube, and frigid but often sun-blinded January can't compare with the sheer monochromatic desolation of February and March—Farch, we call it, for the two months flow together in a gray stew of snow and sleet and mud and despair.

Farch can crack your soul like an egg. Not surprisingly, Farch is suicide season up here. Maybe ending it all seems the only way out for those who can't imagine futures that hold anything more than more of the same and that same not to their liking. I don't know, for in most of my fifty-one winters my mind has been ablaze with a future that springs forth each year like crocuses from beneath the snow, a future where things are never the same and are usually to my liking. For I am, after all, that most unflappably optimistic of all time-wasting windmill tilters, a fly fisherman.

Of course fly fishing isn't proof against craziness. In fact, spending what can easily become serious money and endless time to catch fish you mostly release would by most measures prove craziness.

Bob Hope said that golf unnecessarily prolongs the lives of some of our most useless citizens, and the same could be said of fly fishing. As pastimes go golf seems harmless, unless of course you count the global proliferation of manicured wastelands and grown men wearing yellow shirts and puce plus fours. Still, it could be argued that if golf offends some it at least harms none. Golf balls likely don't mind being whacked with sticks and stuffed down holes. But I'd guess a trout very much minds being dragged to the bank by a steel hook stuck in its jaw, even if it is then wished well and tenderly bade go free.

A certain breed of animal rightist sees fly fishing as little more than a complex version of pulling the wings off flies. Fishing for food is one thing, they archly say, but fishing that serves no purpose beyond self-pleasure is simply unconscionable.

I'd probably agree with them if fly fishing weren't so much fun.

And fly fishing is ever so much fun. For a fly fisher, winters are hardly long enough to hold all the fond looks back toward seasons past and ahead toward those to come—all those fishing trips to remember and those to plan; all those fly boxes to fill with patterns old and new; all those walls to paper over with topographic maps bristling with pushpins and optimistic Post-its distilled from a year's worth of espionage: "Jim says there's a helluva Hendrickson hatch here in May"; and "Try here the first of June: Dan says he caught a six-pounder two years ago and saw one half again as big chasing smelts up this little brook"; and "I think this is the stream D. was talking about in his book; he changed all the names, but everything matches"; and "The new satellite photos show this bridge has been out for four years; hike in there the last of June and camp for a week."

Small wonder the invasion of Normandy, one of the best-planned and most devious military assaults of all time, was masterminded by a fly fisherman.

For a fly fisher, January and February can fly by quickly, filled as they are with readying equipment and studying weighty fishing tomes so numbingly academic you could not be forced to read them for less than a full professorship. But come March, when opening day emerges as a red-circled preview pane on the trout-porn calendar's corner, life slows to a crawl.

Emily Dickinson was so fond of March she invited it upstairs for a chat and locked the door against April, though I suspect she was already dressing only in white and hiding in the attic when she and March tittered together over her maple trees' misreading of the calendar. And she lived south of here, in Massachusetts, where March can indeed stroll in with a springlike bounce in its step. She was right to suspect April as a false friend, though, and so was T. S. Eliot, who knew it for the cruellest month without, so far as I know, even being a fly fisherman.

In most places trout season opens in April, but even where I grew up in the East Tennessee hills, the April opening day was more endured than enjoyed. Even such modern miracles as Polartec and Gore-Tex can't make opening day truly pleasurable, for the fish feed reluctantly if at all, and fight indifferently if at all, and overanxious anglers crowd onto the streams like flies to a piece of green meat.

After years of dredging lead-weighted nymphs past indifferent fish with hands gone numb and gray, I have finally stopped bothering with opening day at all. Life holds enough disappointments to stoke my darker side without joining the madding crowds shivering through the mid-April opening. So I sit at home through false-friend April and bide my time, making lists and dreaming up plans and marking up map after map, and by May it's time to check off those lists and enact those plans, to load the truck and follow those maps to bright sweet rivers, where spruce limbs bow beneath weighty spring drizzle, skunk cabbage spirals from spate-scoured banks, the season's first draggled mayflies tempt trout up from the depths while fiddlehead ferns glow green in the shadows and white-throated sparrows pierce the quiet with a clear pure voice that fills even the most winter-hardened hearts with hope and affection for the world and all it contains.

May is a time of beginnings. And in the North it is time—*the time*—to go fishing.

And should long-awaited expeditions stuffed with a winter's worth of expectations not follow those carefully scripted scores? Well, at least you're fishing. It's important to remember that.

It's funny what you inherit. From my mother I got blue eyes, a love of language, a quick temper, and a master plan for the workings of the world. When the world refused to follow our elaborate plans, then the world could just go to hell and everyone within earshot had to suffer. I say this in the past tense, for I have since walled off those nattering genetic unpleasantries behind psychic bricks and mortar. Mostly.

I still overplan; I can't help it. List making comes as naturally to me as writing with my right hand and falling asleep with a book in my lap. My wife need only suggest a ride to Bangor for supplies and I'm plotting itineraries more appropriate for an assault on Everest than a quick trip to Sam's Club. And should we find ourselves detouring nine miles around road construction or encounter bare shelves where we'd expected to see the industrial vats of Crisco and the feedbags of chocolate chips my grocery list claims we need, I just smile and say, Well, at least we had a nice ride in the country. Honest. These days I never accuse her of conspiring with road crews and stock boys to thwart my grand designs. Well, hardly ever.

I'm embarrassed to admit I used to let this inherited insanity spoil my fishing, too. And not just mine. I remember a trip I planned one fevered January. My friend Malcolm and I would steal from demanding careers a four-day mid-May weekend, launch my new canoe just below Fifth Machias Lake, and make camp four miles downstream at the remains of Knight Dam. We'd fish the rapids there in the evening and morning, then cruise through the rest of the eighteen-mile loop, fishing and camping at carefully X-marked spots along the three shining lakes and interconnecting swift rivers that Edmund Ware Smith wrote about back in the 1950s.

Smith's stories in *Field & Stream* rang with sharp axes, flashing paddles, and the crisp resinous tang of spruce and pine, and they steered me toward Maine as much as anything this side of Thoreau. Thus this trip would be less a fishing expedition than a Pilgrimage, a reverent journey through a wild wet world visited only by intrepid voyageurs such as we.

We shoved off into a warm May afternoon and sped down the thin little river, prying and drawing around rocks, lifting over beaver dams, eddying out to scout rapids, getting the feel of the canoe and of ourselves, seeing en route ducks, beavers, muskrats, deer, ospreys, eagles, pileated woodpeckers, signs of a moose and of a bear—all the things that make wild trout fishing so much more than the mere pursuit of fish. That cirrus tendrils feathered the sky troubled us not a whit; we'd already seen the low heading east on the morning's weather maps. And although we both then led closeted lives as corporate drones, we had both once been commercial lobstermen. Getting wet, we knew, is integral to a life outdoors. And we both also knew how fishing can come alive when bright blue skies turn leaden and spit rain. Rain? Bring her on, by the jaysus.

We arrived at the campsite right on schedule. It was just starting to rain, but a camp was quickly pitched by such woodsmen as we, and a fire neatly built and expertly cooked over and properly stared into.

We hardly slept that night, and it wasn't just anticipation that kept us awake, or the nightlong whippoorwill concert conducted at point-blank range, or the raccoons that ran amok after choking on a plastic-wrapped Brillo pad they mistook for food, or the beaver that kahploonked cannonshot alarms at the canoe parked too near his construction site. We were *cold,* even burrowed into good three-season bags and our entire collection of outerwear.

With a frost-free date of May 20 hereabouts, we expect a little cold even in mid-May. What we didn't expect, when we stumbled from the tent at dawn, was an inch of ice binding the canoe to the shore and stretching three feet into the river, and fat wet snowflakes drifting down on a bitter wind.

It won't last, we agreed. It's freaking *May.* But as we broke camp and chopped the canoe free, the snow and wind ignored logic and the calendar and intensified into a late-winter northeaster, and a winter's worth of anticipation and planning began to fall apart. Paddling five miles through Fourth Lake with the flaccid current but against the stiff wind began to seem less like a scene from Smith's "The One-Eyed Poacher of the Maine Woods" than from Solzhenitsyn's *One Day in the Life of Ivan Denisovich.*

I don't remember whose idea it was to head home. And I don't remember what I said about all this at the time. It's something else walled off behind psychic bricks and mortar.

I don't remember much about that long shivering slog back up-river, either, except that Malcolm poled silently in the stern and I poled loudly in the bow. When we finally got back to the truck, our watch caps had sprouted perfect snow cones and we looked like Conehead canoemen from Remulak. I hope I stopped bitching long enough to laugh.

I don't know whether it was the Conehead expedition to the Machias or the Memorial Day Escape the following May that severed a promising fishing partnership that began when we met at a party to which our respective wives had dragged us. I'd planned both trips, and although I couldn't take blame for the May snowstorm, I could certainly take credit for the events of Memorial Day.

Malcolm and I both faced another overscheduled spring and could squeeze free only Memorial Day weekend—the busiest of the year for Maine anglers. To avoid the crowds, I hatched the scheme of paddling six miles across a popular lake then poling up a remote stream running off a mountain's untrammeled shoulder—a stream, said an article in an old copy of *Outdoor Life,* that was swift, wild, untouched, and absolutely filled with trout and salmon. My topographic map showed no roads within miles.

We were late getting to the lake and, in a freshening northwesterly, late crossing it. And although the stream was indeed swift, wild, and untouched, it was also perfectly featureless, so that instead of poling easily from eddy to eddy we had to get out and wade, dragging the loaded canoe some two miles up a steep inclined plane.

It was almost dark before the fun-park waterslide slowly changed into a boulder-studded trout stream. We made camp by flashlight in a narrow gap in the thick black growth covering both banks.

The next morning we awoke alone amid untouched wilderness on Maine's busiest outdoor weekend, and we rigged rods in a haze of self-congratulatory anticipation. Then we smelled bacon.

We followed our noses around a gentle bend some thirty yards upstream and found the rapids ending at a long still pool beside which sat two elderly men in lawn chairs, eating breakfast and watching red-and-white bobbers. Behind them stood a trim log cabin grown over with the moss of age, and across the stream sat a gleaming new pickup truck.

"How long have this cabin and road been here?" I asked.

"Oh, thutty years, prob'ly," one answered.

"How's the fishing?"

"Oh, used to be pretty good years back. Pretty much gone to hell since the old drivin' dams blew out—lessee, musta been 'long around 1970."

I don't remember exactly what I said after that, although whatever it was I remember saying a lot of it. And I remember it was a quick trip back downstream. And our last trip together.

I write this in January, leaning back with my feet to the woodstove, keeping one eye on a possible blizzard threatening the weekend and another on a calendar seeded with possibilities that begin blossoming in May. For the season's first trip I'll meet a friend for a long weekend on the Rapid River—another pilgrimage of sorts, to the environs of Louise Dickinson Rich of *We Took to the Woods* fame. And should the fishing not be what it once was, or should it rain or snow or be crowded with other anglers drawn to famous water by a long winter's hunger . . . well, at least I'll be fishing, and doing it in a beautiful place and in good company.

Then there's that little brook I spotted dashing under a back road not twenty miles from home. According to the map—a new one, I hasten to add—it wanders fifteen miles through unbroken forest before touching another road. Since last week, when we drove home from the annual L. L. Bean warehouse sale by a roundabout way and saw the perfect little trout stream winding back into thick stands of beech and oak, I've thought of little else but the day in May when I'll load the backpack with three days' provisions and a sleeping bag and tent, and head upstream into the unknown.

Seeds long planted grow wild in the mind, but should the real brook be little more than a dank chain of dead-water sloughs sparsely salted with finger-length troutlings and not the endless escalator of high-stepping plunge pools alive with chunky dark brookies I see in my dreams, I'll swallow my expectations and be happy with whatever this new place may offer. Honest.

Playtime gets ever-shorter shrift in this hectic modern world. It's a crime to spoil what few pleasant moments we can steal by bringing to the water the results-driven expectations of the workplace, turning something meant to be fun into a warped imitation of what we'd hoped to leave behind. In so doing we miss what leads us to the water in the first place: the hope—not the absolute promise—of connecting briefly with another life, and another way of living, through a line cast long months before.

During our progression as anglers we learn to keep our backcasts out of trees, to keep enough slack in our lines to avoid drag but not so much that we miss strikes. We learn where fish live, what they eat, and when they eat it. And during our progression as people we learn about ourselves, out there on the bright spring waters, about what is important and what is not. We learn to take things as they come, and to appreciate being where we are, doing what we're doing. We learn, if we pay attention, that plans are nothing more than the rough outline for a life.

And most of all, we learn that fishing is not meant to be foolproof, but it is meant to be fun.

It's important to remember that.

2

Bumping Bottoms

And all my days are trances,
And all my nightly dreams
Are where thy gray eye glances
And where thy footstep gleams—
In what ethereal dances,
By what eternal streams.

—EDGAR ALLEN POE,
"To One in Paradise"

During the recession that impoverished the early 1970s, I worked in a Bangor camera store that was slowly going belly-up as longtime customers increasingly shopped only for trinkets and advice then mailed their serious money to New York. Long dry hours I spent leaning across the counter, chatting infrequently with regulars who dropped in for coffee and an emergency can of D-76, and talking endlessly and earnestly with my co–sales clerk, a brilliant young

Genevieve Bujold look-alike who had grown up in small-town Maine delightfully unaffected by the name Pandora.

Like me, she was both an ardent angler and an ardent newlywed, and we rambled for hours about these and other shared passions. Once, by mutual consent of our nonfishing and trendily tolerant new spouses, we spent an idyllic day wet-wading a lovely secret stream, where we caught jewel-bright brook trout, an afternoon thunderstorm, and each other's blushing eyes as we fumbled into dry clothing.

I was, I think, a little in love with her, and with the hopeful hindsight of a wistful middle-age male, she with me, though with our happy marriages so recently under way we would never have admitted this to each other or even to ourselves. Still, an electric aura seemed to crackle around us, particularly on those days when the plaid-jacketed, white-belted old gent in the adjoining music store would sit down to fiddle with his Wurlitzer and we, partly as therapy for the customer-free tedium and the jerkily painful polkas, and partly as silent permission to almost innocently touch, broke into a pre-disco-crisis dance called The Bump—a rhythmic riot of colliding rumps and red-faced laughter that sent the clock spinning quickly toward quitting time. As our flesh yielded softly if briefly to the magnetic draw of underlying structure, blue sparks arced from hip to hip.

It reminded us of the springtime ritual of dredging river bottoms with weighted nymphs, we decided, by way of laboring toward safe conversational ground. When you're doing it right, the tickle of a heavy nymph bumping against bedrock bottom flows through leader and line and soft flexible lever directly to the skeletal foundation of your body. You feel every nuance of hidden structure, every tentative tap of nymph against unseen stone or phantom fish against fly. And that elemental electrical contact with the invisible, we agreed, was the key to a solid connection, whether with trout, trout stream, or human.

Before we ourselves could inadvertently connect in less inno-cent ways she moved out of state, she and her bright new husband chasing, like so many young Mainers with a fresh university educa-tion, jobs that don't involve running chain saws or inquiring if there'll be fries with that clam roll. But I never forgot our head-fishing analogy, or the electric thrill of bumping bottoms to the thump of indescribably bad polka music, there behind the silent dusty cash register of a small-town camera store slowly being eutha-nized by economic evolution.

And if you think all this has a very tenuous connection with fly fishing, you've spent too much time dangling your nymphs from indicators.

More often than not I do just that, dangle my nymphs from indi-cators I mean. After all, fishing with weighted nymphs suspended from buoyant strike indicators places few demands on a wandering mind and easily opens distant waters to deep probing. But it is an im-precise practice, especially on those days when foul weather or sulky disposition glues fish tightly against the bottom. No matter how often you adjust an indicator to the preferred one and a half times the water depth, your flies track not the irregular ups and downs of submerged topography but a constant preset distance from the sur-face plane, connecting with the bottom and its electric tickle only by accident.

At one time or another almost every trout fancier trots out the shopworn homily that salmonids feed either on the surface or on the bottom, leaving everything in between a sterile wasteland. I most re-cently heard this from my brother, a bottom bumper of long experi-ence who recited it last spring while nipping a half dozen fat splitshot between a pair of heavily weighted stonefly nymphs as soon as we had drifted downstream from the West Branch Penobscot's fly-fishing-only, no-added-weight zone. When Walter finally felt the familiar tick of nymph on stone, a connection administratively denied him all morning, his face assumed the beatific glow of an expert confident of a hookup.

He got one, too, though with the bottom and not with a fish. But after rerigging—something bottom-bumping nymphmeisters may do a dozen times a day, the shopworn homily here being that if you're not hanging up and losing flies now and then your flies aren't on the bottom—he did in fact connect with a fish, a *big* fish, the biggest one on what turned out to be a phenomenally arid and climatologically disadvantaged trip: a four- or five-pounder. That the deep bend in his rod came not from a slashing salmon or a bulldogging brook trout but from a snuffling sadsack sucker triggered a round of rueful laughter tempered with moral vindication: It may have been a sucker, but at least by God he had finally gotten those lead-mine nymphs of his to tend bottom, no small trick in a river as deep and swift as the Penobscot.

Getting weighted nymphs to the bottom of a deep swift river—I mean *really* to the bottom, where the nymphal forms of stoneflies and mayflies and caddisflies tumble deliciously and helplessly along—is less easily done than you would think. In moving water the current constantly strives to lift your flies from the strike zone, acting not just on the obvious culprits of dragging line and leader but also on the flies themselves.

Drop your big weighted stonefly nymphs into a bucket of still water and they'll root for the bottom like a drilling rig. But drop them into a swift current and they may drift several feet downstream before touching bottom, whether connected to a dragging leader and line or not. All other things being equal, the smaller the fly—and thus the less surface area presented to the hydraulic thrust of current—the faster it will sink to the bottom and the longer it will drift through the skinny strike zone of the sharp pocket water where this brand of fishing is king. A sparse size-sixteen caddis pupa, freighted down with a pair of one-eighth-inch tungsten beads, will be rolling edibly along the bottom at the head of the pocket while the size-six stonefly, with its ten turns of heavy lead fuse wire, glides serenely by far above brief piscine attention spans.

The right materials are as important for effective bottom bumping as a hydrodynamically unobtrusive fuselage. Tungsten beads are roughly three times denser than brass beads and are within a few fractions of the mass of lead. A sparse tungsten beadhead has nowhere to go but down, and a pair of double-tungsten beadhead nymphs with three large splitshot nipped onto the leader between will bore for the bottom at Niagara. Tin shot is roughly half as dense as lead, but lead is environmentally inexcusable and increasingly illegal, and with highly engineered tin shot such as Dinsmore's ovoid Egg Shot, tin's advantages—it's infinitely reusable without losing its shape, it doesn't stick to rock the way lead does, and the teardrop shape that Dinsmore uses makes casting shot-chains almost pleasurable compared with the uncontrollable bolo-toss of round shot—begin to outweigh cheap old reliable lead.

The right techniques are even more important than materials. The late George Harvey devised (or at least named) a cast that sends flies to the bottom like a depth charge. Popularized by Joe Humphreys in his valuable books *Joe Humphreys' Trout Tactics* and *On the Trout Stream with Joe Humpreys* (Stackpole, 1981 and 1989 respectively—absolute must-haves for the serious student of nymphery), the herky-jerky tuck cast is the polar opposite of the fluidly ethereal brand of fly casting designed to flutter wispy dry flies onto the unruffled surface of a pellucid glide. A proper tuck cast is not something you'll see in a life-insurance commercial or a Robert Redford movie. It looks less like the caster is performing aerial ballet than like he's having a seizure.

Make a short, sharp, and very high backcast, then move the rod briskly forward when you feel the heavy nymphs straighten out behind you and stop it high, between ten and eleven o'clock. By stop the rod I mean slam it to a dead-cold stop with an exaggerated snap. The easiest way to do this is drive ahead on the grip with your thumb (the tip of which should be traveling along a straight line toward your target) and pull back sharply with your bottom two fingers; I find I get a quicker stop and fewer tangles if I raise my elbow sharply just as I snap the rod dead still. The flies will shoot ahead as the line loop unrolls, the line will come taut with a jerk, and the flies will snap down below the line tip and arc back toward you, drilling into the water like an osprey. If you twist your wrist to the right or left just as you slam the rod to a stop, you can even make your flies curl a little to the right or left.

You can do the same thing with a roll cast, driving the rod forward straight and hard and lifting your elbow for an abrupt slamming stop. Again, by stop I don't mean a Formula One car slamming on its brakes but a Formula One car slamming into a bombproof missile silo. *Bam,* as Humphreys says in his books. *Stop* that rod—with the rod tip never dropping below ten o'clock.

The idea is, you don't want your leader and flies to straighten out before the line does; this would mean instant drag that will tow your flies past the holding water long before they reach the bottom. Done right, nothing short of a suspension of gravitational laws more effectively connects your flies with the bottom or more efficiently protects them from drag.

For a nymph fisher, which I define as an angler too impatient to wait for a good hatch and therefore easy fishing, the tuck cast is worth perfecting. If you figure out a way to do it with an indicator on your leader, however, please share your powers with the rest of us;

I either get a flaccidly ineffectual tuck or stitch nymphs, shot, and indicator into a cat's cradle.

More often than not I humor my congenital inattention by dangling my nymphs from a bobbing indicator, and I do as well as I feel the need to do, given that I'm fishing for fun and not for food. But on some hard waters and on some tough days, I strip off the bobber and weight my cast until I feel the earth's hard shell through the spider's silk of leader and line. And when my attention isn't wandering to far-off organ music or sweeping the distant shore for a Genevieve Bujold look-alike with an unlikely name whom I hope still bumps bottoms and smiles her endearing chipmunk smile on some trout stream near or far, I'll connect with a solid throbbing life.

Which is, of course, the point of all this.

3

Humility Creek

*Human pride is not worthwhile; there is always
something lying in wait to take the wind out of it.*

—MARK TWAIN,
"Following the Equator"

Great fishing. Like pornography, we all define it differently, but we all know it when we see it. Or think we do.

I've had my share of great fishing: High-mountain freestones with a fat, hungry cutthroat in every pocket. Tropical chum slicks boiling with brutish amberjacks and giant trevally. Wild Arctic rivers where record-book brook trout stripped Muddler after Muddler to the bare hook then took that, too. Remote Maine inlets where landlocked salmon chased spawning smelt like wolves. Backcountry cypress swamps where trash cans with gills hoovered down poppers while alligators looked on with periscope eyes.

But when my backing runs out and I'm flat on my back with tubes up my nose, it won't be reruns of the easy fish flickering across my eyelids. It'll be the fish I worked hard to catch and didn't—fish that humbled a well-read, well-equipped angler of long experience and inquisitive nature, and did so with a brain the size of a green pea.

I began fly fishing as a child and was taught by a master. By my mid-twenties I had read every fly-fishing book I could find and caught fish in Tennessee mountain streams and valley rivers, in the Chesapeake Bay from Cape Henry to Cape Charles, in brooks, rivers, lakes, and ponds the length and breadth of Maine. I had become, in my mind, a certified expert.

When not off on backcountry expeditions I fished my little back-yard trout brook as daily devotions, and I came to know it as well, I told myself, as a brook could be known. Then one bright spring day I made my usual perfunctory pair of casts into a tight elbow where the main current, reinforced by a spring-fed tributary, blasted obliquely against a steep forested esker's muddy heel, swept knee-deep across a smooth gravel plain, then boiled through a notch in a mossy Ordovician ledge slicing diagonally from bank to bank. It was textbook trout habitat, but I'd never seen a fish there. That day, however, something big swirled. When nothing showed to repeated casts, I figured I'd spooked a muskrat.

One parched summer a few years later, while detouring over the ridge to an upstream logjam that I thought might still hold enough water to hide a fish, I looked down into the elbow and saw three forearm-length trout swaying slowly above the gravel. I crept through the interwoven tangle of young spruce toward a casting position, but when my rod poked out from the thicket they dematerialized like Kirk and Spock in the transporter.

I ran back home for a face mask and a flashlight and found, gouged out beneath that shaky mud heel, a cavern the size of a steamer trunk, at the back of which dark torpedic forms pressed tightly against an inverted forest of roots.

I began fishing that elbow obsessively—studying it, analyzing it, drawing three-dimensional plots of its multilayered currents—until one wild spring when floods tore through and relieved the cavern of its roof. All my obsessing never earned me a touch, although every now and then, on magical misty spring afternoons with march browns lumbering aloft, I would catch a brief, rippled glimpse of big, secretive trout. When I close my eyes I can see them still.

In the intervening quarter century I've been humbled by the best: a football-fat Magalloway landlock that nudged aside my perfect Parachute Hendrickson to take a real *Ephemerella subvaria* floating alongside; an enormous flame-yellow brown that hydroplaned up a thin Madison River channel and tore a foot-long rainbow from my line, and which spent the next week sneering at the big trouty streamers I puppeteered past his lair; a jaded Slough Creek cutthroat so annoyed by the parade of imitations I kept plopping amid his stash of helicoptering stoneflies that he charged down my line with flaring fins and snapping jaws.

Over the uneven path leading from my brash twenties to the theoretical wisdom of middle age, I like to think that these fish and others like them have permanently lanced an ego swollen by fishing mostly to easy fish, and replaced it with a proper reservoir of humility.

But last year, at one of those tackle-company soirees where the season's latest toys are served up with trout fishing and T-bones and low-key lobbying for favorable press, I ran afoul of a fish with a whole new way of imposing perspective. The last day of the conference my friend Jim and I dodged the dog-and-pony show and an organized field trip into Yellowstone and snuck off to Nelson's Spring Creek, where the lodge, we'd learned, had a couple of vacant rods that day.

I'd never fished Nelson's, a fertile natural fish hatchery of world-wide reputation that has been well and thoroughly flogged by some of the keenest and most experienced fly fishers who have ever lived. But like almost everyone else with fly fishing on the brain I desperately wanted to fish Nelson's, in the same way a journeyman actor might long to perform *King Lear* at the new Globe or a budding ballerina dance *Giselle* at the Mariinsky.

It was about what I expected: lovely and lush and as intimidating as a Parris Island obstacle course. Beneath burning Big Sky sunshine, custardy clots of pea-green algae slid down shining sheets of crystalline water, below whose braided surface cress jungles undulated and tubby trout sipped indifferently at legions of scuds and sow bugs like Romans nibbling grapes at an orgy. To make casting interesting, restless winds gusted from five to twenty-five knots and wandered randomly around the compass. In midafternoon the pale morning duns began hatching, then thought better of it.

I managed to take a couple of small and doubtless very stupid fish on minute emergers late in the morning and another pair of easy midsized trout during the brief PMD hatch, and for forty-five minutes I cast to a good cutthroat that relocated his feeding lane every time one of my flies drifted near, until with the help of a properly circumspect guide I finally hit the right fly and the right approach and the right lull in the wind and took him, too.

It was a hard day on hard-fished water, and I was pretty proud of myself even though Jim caught a dozen or better over the same time. But then he's one of those eagle-eyed fish hawks of wide and catholic experience, and I'm a mere featherheaded writer who feels truly at home only on small upcountry freestone streams full of dumb little wild trout and who even at the most demanding of times tends to, as we used to say in the Olden Days, space out.

After a late lunch I headed downstream, looking for spots the highly educated spring-creek specialists who probe these waters might have missed, places where a freestoner like me might luck into a good trout. Finally, at the tail of one deep run, in a gap in the cress tight against the bankside path, I spotted a brief flicker of white and a long black ripple: a big anthracite-colored brown enjoying the constant crustaceal banquet that inflates spring-creek trout like dirigibles and make them not so much selective of artificials as simply uninterested.

I dropped off the path and circled around through the cotton-woods, then slithered through the grass like Wyeth's Christina reaching out for her world until I was ten feet off the brown's port quarter. Lying prone, I crossarmed a tiny olive scud about fifteen feet upstream of his lie, and the fly drifted down the current straight into his mouth. I tightened the line and felt his weight, then I stood and cleared for action, expecting two feet of angry brown trout to erupt wildly up the run.

Instead he flicked his head twice against the pull of the line, then swam slowly and deliberately around a clump of cress and a big curd of algae, drew the leader tight, and casually popped it with a twitch of his head. Thus freed, he swam back to his feeding station with an aura of magnificent indifference and resumed picking off scuds and sow bugs, thoroughly unconcerned that a sophisticated FisherMan stood three feet away with his mouth agape, thinking, It's one thing for a trout to reject an offering and quite another for him to scorn your existence as apex predator.

I suspect a steady diet of spring-creek trout would eventually turn me to bird-watching or golf, but Datus Proper, author of *What the Trout*

Said, the most useful book on trout fishing since Ray Bergman's *Trout,* seems to survive a daily dose of it with his psyche intact. He calls the little spring creek running past his Bozeman-area home Humility Creek, in recognition of its consistent ability to crush egos. Nick Lyons, who has fished it, tells me it's "very small water with very large, very skittery trout."

I've got a standing invitation to come fish there, and I hope to do so soon, for a few months after Jim and I fished Nelson's we ended up on the headwaters of Maine's Kennebec River, where in the flush of the prespawn I had my most productive couple of days ever—so many big brook trout and landlocks that I lost count, including an elephantine salmon that took a deep-drifted little caddis pupa and a five-pound brookie that flipped off a tiny Pheasant Tail right at my feet.

Soon I'll have convinced myself I'm really good at this and completely forgotten that I was simply in the right place at the right time, fishing to unnatural concentrations of fish at their least wary time of the year.

I'll be ready for another preventive dose of humility. With artificially inflated egos running rampant through fly fishing's incarnation du jour, it's something we all could use.

4

Tales of the Vienna Sausages

You needn't tell me that a man who doesn't love oysters and asparagus and good wines has got a soul, or a stomach either. He's simply got the instinct for being unhappy highly developed.

—SAKI, *The Chronicles of Clovis*

I was kneeling bedside in my Doctor Dentons and just about through my now-I-lay-me's when the explosion rocked the house. It went on forever, or so it seemed: an endless tooth-grinding shriek, the likes of which I would not hear again until Jimi Hendrix stuffed his Stratocaster through a stack of Marshall amps levitating thirty feet from my tender teenage ears and left me forever after saying, Huh?

As the cowboy-and-Indian wallpaper lit up with the orange glow of distant flames, I looked up at my mother's sampler—a needlework scene of two small boys kneeling at prayer in the remains of their bombed-out house while a cross of bombers loomed overhead, which she had thought might comfort two small boys trying to fall asleep twenty-three miles from the Oak Ridge atom-bomb plant at the height of the Cold War. My eyes filled with tears as I read again the words she'd stitched thereon: Now I lay me down to sleep, I pray the Lord my soul to keep. If I should die before I wake, I pray the Lord my soul to take.

I thought it unfair of the Lord to be taking my soul before I even got to sleep, never mind reached my eighth birthday, but who was I to complain? Life, I knew from reading the Bible and the *Knoxville News Sentinel,* is usually unfair. And after almost eight years of looking up at that sampler, I was pretty sure my years upon the earth would be numbered in single digits. At least, I figured, I'd finally be able to get some sleep up there in heaven, assuming I wasn't brought to judgment for braining my brother with a building block or stealing my father's Chesterfields.

But the Lord came that night not to take away souls but to bring what most of the town saw as manna from heaven, for the explosion wasn't the sneak attack of Godless Communists envious of our Bibles and televisions and indoor plumbing but rather a Southern Railways redball that had jumped the tracks at fifty miles an hour and torn down the side of a local freight at the siding just outside town.

I don't remember if anyone was hurt. I only remember a tangle of twisted wreckage over which the townsfolk flitted like crows on a roadkill, filling baskets and pillowcases with the cans of Vienna sausage that peppered a mile of mainline; the local had loaded up but good at the meatpacker four towns down the line, and the redball had taken that line of The-Southern-Serves-The-South boxcars at its word and opened it like a tin of sardines.

The Lord provides His bounty in mysterious ways. It would be years before we'd need to buy another fishing-trip lunch.

Vienna sausages are the cornerstone of southern fishing lunches: an ostensible comestible with the pinky gray ooziness of a suicide's spattered brains, the Upton Sinclair savor of an abattoir's clotted drains, the shuddery shape of little boner dog dicks drowned in jellied lymph.

The can I have here before me says it contains Mechanically Separated Chicken, Beef Tripe, Partially Defatted Cooked Beef Fatty Tissue, Beef Hearts, Water, Partially Defatted Cooked Pork Fatty Tissue, Salt, and less than 2 percent of the following popular household condiments: Mustard, Natural Flavorings, Dried Garlic, Vinegar, Dextrose, Sodium Erythorbate, and Sodium Nitrite.

I'm happy not knowing what Sodium Erythorbate is, but as a thirty-year resident of what was until recent hard times the Poultry Capital of the Northeast, I inadvertently know that Mechanically Separated Chicken is made by forcing scraps of demeated chicken carcasses through a sieve. Just scrape off what viscous remnants ooze through and there's your primary ingredient in Vienna sausages.

It's been years since I've eaten one. I remember them being salty, fatty, and ferrous. But memories are unreliable witnesses, so by way of journalistic research I tried a bit of the can I bought this morning. I plopped a pinky gray sausage on a saltine just as we used to years ago for a streamside lunch, and the taste remains the same: an initial burst of garbage-disposal grease followed by a salty metallic aftertaste that leaves your mouth puckered and sour, as though you'd upchucked chunks of green persimmon then fellated a rusty exhaust pipe.

I dwell on all of this partly from the morbid fascination that attracts humans to highway carnage and partly because it leads me into what I'm told writing teachers call a "thesis," which the dictionary says is a "dissertation advancing an original point of view as a result of research."

- My research: eating Vienna sausages with a mature and educated palate.
- My original point of view: Most fishing lunches are mere gastrointestinal afterthoughts that poison what is meant to be a pleasant day astream.

And there's no need for this. Anyone who can spend endless hours tying perfect Pheasant Tails, perfecting arcane fly-casting techniques, and agonizing over complex leader formulae can damn well find a better lunch to tuck in the fishing vest than a can of Vienna sausages and a Ziploc of crumbling saltines.

Take, for example, the French sandwich known as the *pan bagnat*. According to Jacques Pepin's and Julia Child's *Cooking at Home,* pan bagnat means "bathed bread," because in Niçoise, where the pan bagnat originated, the sandwich is "lavishly drenched with olive oil and vinaigrette," so much so that "the local people would say it isn't any good unless the oil drips down your arm and off your elbow while you're eating it!" Which makes it a prime candidate for a real fishing lunch. Especially for a southerner.

To make a pan bagnat, you need a good hard roll or a small focaccia, store bought or homemade. Slit the bread in half so it opens like a hamburger bun, saturate both top and bottom with a couple of tablespoons of extra-virgin olive oil, then layer on Stuff until you can't layer on any more Stuff—Stuff being defined as whatever you can find that looks edible, though the bulk of Stuff should be saladesque. Usually I dress half a head of romaine with a mustard-garlic vinaigrette, then layer on thin slices of various cheeses, roasted garlic, canned tuna or leftover meat, chopped black olives, thin-sliced seeded tomatoes, and canned anchovies, then I drizzle more vinaigrette over everything before topping it all off with the rest of the bread.

Now here's where an outsized sandwich not even Dagwood could wrap his jaws around becomes a fly fisher's vest-packed dream: Bundle this mess tightly in two layers of plastic wrap, set it on a plate, set another plate on top, balance on top of this a heavy pan with added weight, and leave it in the refrigerator overnight. By morning the sandwich will have compressed into a magnificent monocoque structure that nestles happily in your vest and, because the contents are preserved in oil almost like a confit, is impervious to any injury that won't kill you, too. When you're ready for lunch, slice it up and go to it.

I ran across my first pan bagnat in Québec when my fishing tackle and I were driving around the Gaspé Peninsula. To me the sadsack sandwiches in the *dèpanneur*'s cooler looked like old BLTs trampled by an elephant, but the nice lady at the cash register kept insisting I try one and was too charming and insistent to resist. About five miles down the road I unwrapped it and took an experimental bite, then I turned around and drove back and bought two more. She said, as she took my money, "Ah-ha-*haaaaaa*," nodding her head and skinning her eyebrows up and down exactly as you would expect of a vindicated Frenchwoman who looked to have spent at least a portion of her distant youth wearing fishnet stockings, a short skirt, and a beret.

Making a pan bagnat is a job of work if you're not, as we used to say back in the sixties, Into Food. But even the shiftless can find better lunch choices than Vienna sausages, a prime example being the sardine. The can I have before me was packed in Belfast, Maine, only six miles from where I sit. The ingredients read Sardines, Soybean Oil, Salt—simple and elegant and free of polysyllabic carcinogens and slaughterhouse secretions. And sardines are even good for you, if you're the nervous sort who cares about such things. Like olive oil, oily fish like sardines boost your good cholesterol and reduce your bad cholesterol. Good and bad cholesterols have real names—something to do with HDL and LDL or LDS or something like that—but I can never keep straight which one does what, and I no longer pay attention to those weekly nutritional studies that start with an answer then sniff backward for supporting evidence.

Back when I lobster fished for a living I ate sardines for lunch every day, in part because I could buy them cheaply by the case from the same cannery that sold me my bait, and in part because the odor of that bait—lobsters are lured into traps by a mesh bag stuffed with a softball-sized wad of salted herring cuttings, herring being what a sardine was before a lady wearing a hair net snipped off its stern half and stuffed it into a can and sent its bow half down a chute to the bait tank—never quite leaves your hands. Because anything I ate would taste of herring anyway, I reasoned, why ruin a good ham sandwich? With sardines for lunch, washing up was as easy as trailing my hands briefly over the side of the boat.

For sport fishers, sardines for lunch may have another advantage, for sardines are, of course, little fish. And as everyone knows, big fish eat little fish. Woolly Buggers that accidentally drop into open sardine cans then get accidentally swept under cutbanks have a way of snaking out enormous and heretofore uncatchable brown trout. Or so I hear.

But there's more to streamside cuisine than extracting something from a can and balancing it on a saltine or even manufacturing a magnificently impervious sandwich, the most obvious and sublime choice being—to edge circuitously into my real thesis—lunching on a couple of the lithe little fish that bring us streamside in the first place.

In these days of I Don't Like It So Don't You Do It, countless fly fishers have never known the simple pleasures of knocking a couple of little trout on the head and broiling them over a tiny streamside fire. Some, in fact, recoil in horror at the very thought.

With America's hungry millions doubling in my lifetime and spreading out across the countryside like bacteria in a petri dish, and trout streams suffering everywhere from acid rain and riverside development and sheer weight-of-numbers overfishing—yes, even politically correct catch-and-release kills fish if done incautiously, and in heavily fished streams with lots of hold-it-higher-toward-the-camera Kodak moments it kills a *lot* of fish—I don't knock near as many wild trout on the head as I once did, probably no more than a dozen or so a year. But trout fishing would for me lose much of its savor and most of its point if I didn't at least now and then follow the original object of fishing to its logical conclusion, especially in spring, when a long winter's drought must be forcibly flushed away with a suitable tonic.

Lee Wulff's dictum that a gamefish is too valuable to be caught only once is certainly true on the several hundred blue-ribbon rivers thick with heavily advertised outfitters, but across the country there are hundreds of thousands of wayside and wilderness streams and ponds that may go days, months, or even years without seeing an angler. Eating a small trout or two from these unfrequented waters will neither carve irreparable holes in a threatened population nor extract dollars from the pocket of an outfitter who has appropriated a public resource, but it may well help connect an occasional angler with what it is we actually do. Fishing is a bloodsport, no matter how fervently the fly-fishing industry wishes to portray it otherwise.

So societally shunned has the streamside trout lunch become that new-generation fly fishers seem not even to know how to go about it. It couldn't be simpler.

It begins with catching a couple of trout—which is simple enough but fraught with hidden stipulations, the first being the local laws about bag limits, size limits, and fire building. Once the written laws are satisfactorily digested, it's time to question yourself following the unwritten laws that separate a sublime streamside sacrament from the mere harvest of meat. First, have you seen other anglers today? Are bankside paths beaten down like shortcuts between a high school and a hamburger stand, or are they closely overgrown with few signs of passage? Does the stream/pond/lake/river teem with life? Turn over some rocks: Are insects everywhere? Do the shallows swirl with tiny troutlings? More important: Have you been catching enough fish all morning to make you smile, or have fish been few and far between? Are they all about the same size, or did some bigger ones rise to your fly and bring your heart into your throat? Does it seem, after assimilating the evidence, that you've spent the morning on a healthy ecosystem with few other predators and plenty of trout? Or even, if all the trout are about the same size, an overgrown tree of life in want of pruning? Then what possible harm could there be in turning predator yourself and lunching on a trout or two? Certainly a couple of eight-inch trout toasted on a stick are far less of a loss to a stream's bottom-loaded gene pool than a fertile two-footer mummified on an office wall as dead testament to your stiff rod.

To do this right, you need to catch lunch no more than an hour before lunch. Any earlier than that and you may find the stream a less copious cornucopia than you'd thought and dip too eagerly from a skinny population. Worse, if you take fish any more than an hour before lunch, you won't be cooking the real-deal *fresh* trout that is essential to this ritual but some sad wilted simulation that tastes little better than something found stiffened on supermarket ice. The closer the death to cooking time, the fresher and better the trout. If gamefish are too valuable to be caught only once, then gamefish like trout are too valuable to be eaten without respect. If it's a hot day, even an hour is too long a wait.

Knock your victim quickly on the head with a knife butt or a stone. In a just world, people who toss trout into a creel to slowly suffocate would be shot on sight. Of course no one really carries creels anymore, so you'll have to improvise a carrying method. I wrap trout in wet ferns—the evaporation keeps them cool and moist—and stick them in one of my vest's outside mesh pockets, where air freely circulates. Whatever you do, don't stuff a trout inside a plastic bag, where it will begin to develop off tastes before you can say anaerobic decomposition. Dress trout you intend to eat immediately after catching them. Always.

Since so many recent converts to fly fishing never learned how to dress trout properly, here's how it's done: Hold the cold-cocked trout belly-up, slip a sharp knife into its vent, and slice quickly and shallowly until you reach the V at the base of the gills. Now lift out the blade and stick it in the soft skin between the lower jaw and the gill plate, and slide it all around the lower jaw, cutting loose the tongue and the lower section of the gills. Put your knife away, stick your left thumb in the trout's lower jaw, and force your right index finger into the gills just below your thumb and down into the body cavity, ripping out the guts and gills all the way down to the vent; deftly done, the belly fins and a slim shard of belly meat will come along for the ride. Toss the guts up into the bushes for the raccoons to find. Slosh the trout around in running water, and as you do this dig out the kidney—the clotted bloody-looking stuff along the apex of the rib cage—with your thumbnail until it's all gone.

If all this sounds disquietingly barbaric in these days of catch-and-release-as-state-religion, perhaps you'd care to accompany me to a slaughterhouse, where we can watch as the sticker and the gutter and the scalder and the scraper and the splitter and the cutter prepare your pork chops for tomorrow night's supper. Or let's go to sea and watch a swordfisherman underrun his longline, slatting off the un-marketable species to sink dead into the depths and hauling aboard immature swordfish five years and fifty pounds shy of even thinking about perpetuating their dwindling species.

Welcome to the top of the food chain.

With two small dressed trout in hand, it's time to build a fire, although I often build my fire first and then go try to catch my trout, being both an overconfident angler and a firm believer in the fresher the trout the better the trout.

Cooking over an open fire is another ancient skill fading swiftly from our collective consciousness. Should you sit quietly near a modern campground and watch cookfires built on a bonfire scale—decorative aluminum pans smelting over naked flames, prime steaks vaporizing in electric blue flashes, gobbets of blackened raw indigestion served forth as culinary triumphs—you'd conclude this business of cooking with fire was still in its infancy. But we've already learned all there is to learn. We've just forgotten it.

It's a matter of scale. A proper cookfire is almost laughably small. I build mine at the edge of the stream, far away from peaty forest soils underlain with subterranean roots that burn like secret fuses and explode days later as red devouring demons.

I find a bread-loaf-sized rock for a fireback and roll two smaller rocks downwind and parallel—a tiny π of a fireplace no bigger than your hat that concentrates heat and channels in air like a blowtorch.

Against the fireback I lay a few thin curls of birch bark or dead grass gathered together and tied in a knot, along with some shavings peeled off a dry stick with a sharp penknife and a handful of pencil-thin twigs tepeed together with pencil-wide spaces between to boost the flow of oxygen—the most essential element of the fire maker's triumvirate of fuel and air and heat, and the one most often forgotten. Over that, and leaning against the fireback so it doesn't collapse like a house of cards, I lay a sparse latticework of dry hardwood sticks no bigger than shotgun barrels that I've snapped off downed trees— not those sticks lying on the ground, where moisture migrates within cellular walls and turns sharp clean flame to dull cloying smoke, but those that reach toward the sun.

If I'm carrying my tea pail I fill it with river water and prop it atop the rocks. A quick scrape of the match and a blossom of orange, then without a single wasted BTU the flames spread quickly across the pail's bottom.

When the kettle boils and the fire looks almost dead, it's time to begin cooking in earnest. I peel the bitter bark from a couple of green sticks, sharpen one end, thrust it through a trout's mouth and bury it in the aft end of the rib cage, then do the other. I salt and pepper the cavities from a film can carried in my vest, then with a couple of well-placed rocks I cantilever the trout-on-sticks just in front of but not quite over the coals—fat dripping onto the fire produces black oily smoke that smothers the trout's delicate flavor. Turn them every so often, and in less than ten minutes they should be done—a knife blade near the backbone will tell you when the flesh is just beginning to flake. Overcooking trout is as unpardonable a sin as overeating them.

After lunch I douse the fire, scrape the ashes into the stream, turn the rocks' soot-blackened faces down and out of view, lounge about listening to the endless burble of river music, and contentedly scan the riffle for the opening stanzas of the afternoon hatch.

A couple of small fresh trout crisply broiled over coals. A piece of crusty bread to hold them like a plate and soak up all their juices. A fine pear. Maybe a small flask of *vin ordinaire* cooled in the stream. A couple of miniature York Peppermint Patties to finish things off properly. A constant streamborne symphony playing in the background.

How does lunch get better than that? It isn't an everyday lunch but a special one, a rare treat in these days of rampant population growth, industrialized fly fishing, and transferable guilt. A lunch well worth indulging in, now and then, to remind us that we are part of the web of life and not distant observers.

As Jean Anthelme Brillat-Savarin wrote in *The Physiology of Taste* way back in 1825, "Tell me what you eat, and I will tell you what you are." I, for one, would far rather be a sweet wild trout crisping slowly over coals than a priapic little sausage. So nourished, my soul can then ascend or descend or simply evaporate as it chooses, having enjoyed to the fullest its brief stay in a world where trout swim free, are always loved, and are occasionally eaten.

Second Movement

Summer

Sumer is ycomen in,
Loude sing cuckou!
Groweth seed and bloweth meed,
And springth the wode now.
Sing cuckou!

—Middle English ballad

5

If one does not understand a person, one tends to regard him as a fool.

— CARL JUNG,
"Mysterium Coniunctionis"

$\mathscr{I}$t was a typical summer scene in midcoast Maine. The cold, fertile waters overflowed with mackerel, an annual gift of high-quality protein for vast numbers of hungry predators—ospreys and eagles, bluefish and stripers, seals and porpoises, and, of course, humans. At daybreak a crowd of latter-day hunter-gatherers crowded elbow to elbow onto the Searsport town wharf, looking to the incoming tide for a free meal.

We were a representative cross section of modern American society: wizened old geezers doddering through another in a long chain of seasons; convivial middle-aged matrons in neon caftans and clanking costume jewelry; hormonally addled adolescents in large trousers and reversed ballcaps; sad-eyed men wearing faded uniforms from factories long since sold overseas; prosperous summer people wearing crisp new shorts, expensive wingtips, and constipated expressions.

As anglers we divided into two camps: those who fished with bait and those who did not. Curiously enough, the morning's undisputed highliner was in the much smaller artificial-lure camp and, congenitally incompetent summer complaints excepted, seemed the least likely person on the pier to clean our collective clocks. He was a garrulous individual of amorphous shape—a soft-serve ice cream sculpture of Buddha extruded into lavender-plaid polyester trousers that didn't quite meet his COED NAKED TRUCK DRIVING T-shirt. He talked constantly to everyone who would listen and many who would not, interrupting his monologue only long enough to winch in another hefty mackerel and toss it into the presumably clean ninety-weight gear-oil bucket rapidly filling by his side.

I set down my spinning rod—you will forgive me if I hang up my fly rod long enough to snatch a couple cannerloads of mackerel from a crowded pier where even the most circumspect backcast would be an antisocial act, and where I hope to learn something that will, I feel, have direct relevance to fly fishing—and set about studying this creature and his strange success. His equipment held no secrets. Like the rest of us on the pier, he was using a generic open-face spinning outfit. Like most of the Artificialites, he fished an unadorned diamond jig, flinging it out and jerking it back with numbing monotony.

Next to him stood a razor-thin bundle of well-groomed intensity equipped with expensive but well-used tackle—clearly a serious angler of some experience growing ever more serious each time the loudmouthed highliner, whom I will hereinafter refer to as Phlegm, caught another good mackerel and the quivering bundle of silent intensity—let's call him Spleen—did not.

Scent, I almost said out loud, remembering a magazine article I had started but not finished at the dentist's office the day before. *I'll bet it's scent.* After all, Spleen's blond hair and blue eyes placed him in that unfortunate group whose epidermal oils contain the highest percentage of the amino acid L-serine—a substance proven to repel fish in even the most minute concentrations. Phlegm's darker complexion put him at the other end of the L-serine scale. Was Phlegm cleaning up because he was, so to speak, a natural fisherman? Because Spleen's L-serine-tainted lure stank of Man and Spleen's did not?

But the effects of L-serine can be mitigated in part by a thorough cleansing of the hands, I remembered. And Spleen was fastidious—Felix Unger with a fishing rod. Phlegm was dirty as a hog but not half so appealing. Besides, just how much scent can a chrome-plated hunk of lead retain? If anything, Phlegm's diamond jig should have smelled of terrified mackerel—hardly an attractant for another mackerel. And if scent was the key, why was Phlegm catching not only more fish but also much bigger fish than even those anglers using shrimp, clams, and cutbait? As fond as I was of the scent theory, I finally had to let it go.

Setting aside the question of bait for a moment, could technique make the difference? Their identical diamond jigs flew out the same twenty or so yards and plunked into the water only a few feet apart, and they both retrieved in the classic Germanic oompah-band tempo—*jerk* crank crank, *jerk* crank crank, *jerk* crank crank, *jerk* crank crank—of the seasoned mackerel fisherman.

As you would expect from someone so results-driven, Spleen focused like a laser on the juncture of line and water, looking for even the slightest evidence of a strike. Phlegm seemed to pay no attention to his lure at all. Like everyone else using artificials, he jerked and cranked, jerked and cranked—but at random intervals he paused to refuel with a mixture of cheap cigars, peanut butter crackers, and generic beer, the atomized remains of which spewed forth in a great cloud that accompanied his running commentary on automobiles he had known and loved, and women he had—and this is as distressing to write about as it was to hear—known and loved.

Then Spleen and I both noticed something significant: Almost every one of Phlegm's interruptions produced a fish. Spleen began pausing in his retrieve, too, allowing his jig to fall slack at random intervals. When his hookup rate didn't noticeably improve he became even angrier, concentrated even more furiously, and his oompah band flogged itself into a lederhosen-slapping frenzy. Still no fish. Finally Spleen surrendered, spun on his heel, and fumed off the pier. Phlegm turned and watched him go, smirking and nonchalantly striking another fish.

Then I noticed what Spleen had not: Although Phlegm stopped his retrieve at random and seemed to pay no attention whatsoever to his rod, he was never out of touch with his jig. As he turned to spray a neighbor with cracker crumbs and beer and the sage advice that, although you *could* stuff a fitty-eight Odes-mobeel weah-end into a fitty-five Shevvy, it was shoe-ah as shit gonna chattah wike a fwiggah, his rod tip fell at the precise rate at which his jig sank; his line's catenary curve didn't vary by a minute of arc. He gripped the rod forward of the reel with the line running lightly over his little finger, like an orb-spinning spider resting a leg on its web, feeling for the first tentative touch of a tangled fly. As I watched he struck, seemingly at random, and *boom:* another mackerel.

I cast out my jig, jerked and cranked, jerked and cranked, then let it fall deep, following it down with the rod tip and trailing the line across my little finger—the nerve endings of which, unlike the index finger, are not entombed beneath a layer of work-hardened callus. I felt the barest tickle in the line, snapped back the rod, and was fast to my biggest fish of the day. Again I cast out, jerked and cranked, jerked and cranked, then let it fall. This time as I followed the jig down, the tension on my little finger lessened ever so slightly, as though the jig's descent had hesitated. I set the hook and had another mackerel.

Across the pier our eyes met, Phlegm and I—brothers of the angle sharing an unspoken bond and identical thoughts: Geeze, that asshole ain't nowheres near as stupid as he looks.

And this brings me around to fly fishing, and the lessons to be learned from the unlikeliest sources. The first and most obvious is, What happens when a fish takes a fly? For years angling writers have waxed on about slashing strikes and savage hits, the kind of testosterone-sodden copy that citybound desk editors believe readers want to see. Only on the prissier levels of trout fishing is it permissible to describe a fish's strike in more accurate terms without being blue-penciled into something more assertive: "The huge brown," most of us fly-fish writers have tapped out at one time or another, "delicately sipped the tiny emerger from the film." *Sipped* is good—descriptive but not precisely accurate. *Gulped,* as in the Gulpers of Montana's Hebgen Lake, is closer to the truth. If we wish to be both accurate and evocative we can say inhaled. If we wish to be merely accurate, we can say sucked.

Toothy terrorists like pike and bluefish excepted, the typical gamefish strike has less in common with the carnivorous lunge of a lion attacking a tethered goat than with a Dustbuster assaulting a housefly. If you really want to study the striking moment of gamefish, including those oh-so-prissy trout, get a bug light and a Hoover.

Or you can shanghai, as I did, a small school of fish for lab rats. After digesting the wisdom of Phlegm, I spent several days facedown on a floating dock studying a cooperative class of mixed-species sunfish and smallmouth bass that live conveniently nearby. My lab equipment consisted of a plastic bucket fitted with a Plexiglas bottom, the cloth hood from an old view camera, an assortment of defanged flies and small jigs, miscellaneous insect life gleaned from the garden, and the tip section of a fly rod strung with four-pound-test monofilament.

This wasn't really a Quixotic quest to determine which lures are most attractive to fish—although for the record my unrepresentative sampling preferred a dramatically drowning grasshopper followed by a tiny chartreuse Mister Twister and a sparse size-twelve Beadhead Woolly Bugger. My goal was to observe firsthand how fish eat and, by extension, how better to detect those subtle strikes most of us get without ever knowing we get them.

As a new lure sank beneath the surface the bass would rush forward aggressively and eye it briefly; then the alpha individual would quickly schlurp it in. The sunfish would sidle up to a lure, inspecting it suspiciously, then one would ease forward and tentatively sip it like a debutante eating her first raw oyster. Both species spat out hard lures—tiny spoons, small spinners, leadhead jigs—almost as quickly as they went in. Soft lures—soft plastics with a hook but no leadhead and flies tied primarily from fur and soft feathers—they mouthed briefly before spitting out. With hook-free natural baits it was a quick inhalation, a couple of perfunctory chews, and a swallow, with one exception: An earthworm experimentally skewered on a hook shank clipped at the bend got sucked in then spat out in a fraction of a second.

Everything happened in a fraction of a second. As I danced the lures and flies past the dock I rarely felt anything like a strike, despite the sensitive, short-range connection between rod and lure. Most of the time I felt nothing at all, even though I could clearly see the fish suck in and eject a fraud. Usually the only evidence of a strike was an almost imperceptible slackening or tightening of the line. Only about 20 percent of all takes featured the classic tug, which explains why I miss so many fish drifting a pair of soft-hackle wet flies on a slack line.

By far the most effective action was the rhythmic rise and fall of classic jigging, whether the lure was a jig or a beadhead nymph. Unfortunately, most of the strikes—excuse me, sucks—went undetected because they happened when the lures were falling on a slack line. Some fish trying to suck in a retrieved lure couldn't overcome the pull of the line; this even happened with retrieved natural baits. Far fewer strikes occurred while the lure was being lifted or retrieved, yet most could be detected at the rod. Had I not been following the proceedings under water, I would have concluded that most underwater strikes come on the retrieve, which wasn't the case.

But I did conclude that the fly fisher's favorite multipurpose greeting/benediction, Tight Lines, is more curse than blessing. A tight line is the last thing you want if you would connect with all those fish that take your underwater flies unseen. What you want is a line just loose enough to allow free movement of the fly and just tight enough to transmit the slightest change in tension, although I doubt Limp Lines will ever catch on as a way to sign Christmas cards to fellow fishers.

Nonetheless, here are some findings from my decidedly unscientific research into the Mystery of Phlegm:

- With retrieved underwater flies, you'll likely notice less than 20 percent of the halfhearted strikes you don't know you're getting. To improve hookup percentages, periodically introduce controlled amounts of slack to allow a suspicious fish to suck in the fly, but not so much slack that you miss the message. There's a fine line between the two—like not burning toast.
- With floating flies, if you're paying attention you'll see every strike, but fewer than half those bass and sunfish bothered to come to the surface for a dry fly, half of those didn't strike, and a

full third didn't even bother to come up for floating live bait like a grasshopper. On the other hand, not one underwater presentation failed to elicit at least one take.

- When dead-drifting a pair of wet flies or lightly weighted nymphs on a slack line, hold your rod at a forty-five-degree angle and keep the flies just slightly under tension—you want less a dead drift than a dazed drift; natural insects move slightly in the current as they struggle to regain the bottom, and a line slightly under tension tends to animate flies in a most realistic fashion. You want the flies drifting freely in the current, but you want to see or feel the slightest hesitation in the leader or change in the catenary curve of the line. And be ready to strike instantly with a quick strip of the line hand, if you're the kind of self-possessed individual who can quell the automatic urge to strike with the rod tip and thereby snatch the flies unnaturally from their drift.

- In most cases the commotion made by struggling live bait brings fish from a long way off, and so does a fly that creates a commotion under water, such as a clipped-head Muddler or a big bushy Woolly Bugger. Research (not mine; real scientists) has shown that predators lurking near schools of baitfish target for execution all individuals that look or behave differently—a characteristic all predatory life-forms share, as we can all confirm by thinking quickly back to seventh grade. Larger fish often hang beneath the main school looking for stragglers. And this is how Phlegm, with his erratically dropping diamond jig, caught more large fish than the bait fishers, whose baits hung stationary and uninterestingly beneath their bobbers.

A year later I headed back to the town wharf for another cannerload of mackerel. All the usual suspects were exactly where I'd left them, leaning against the same pilings, wearing the same clothes, talking to the same people about the same things, staring at red-and-white bobbers or casting out and jerking back: *jerk* crank crank, *jerk* crank crank, *jerk* crank crank, *jerk* crank crank.

I nodded to Phlegm, and he nodded back.

"Winter good?" he asked.

"Fair to middlin'. Wasn't much of a winter. How's the fishin'?"

"Spotty. *Oi* ain't done too bad, but they're comin' slow for ever'body else," he said, nodding at his gear-oil bucket half full of fat mackerel, then sweeping his head significantly at the near-empty buckets dotted up and down the pier.

I cast out and retrieved Phlegm-style, and on my third cast landed a nice one.

Phlegm nodded again. "Good fish," he said. "You learn quick."

"You remember that skinny old guy with the wingtips who was here last summer?" I asked. "Seen him this year?"

"Feller't lived down Cottage Street? He was down here all last summer and didn't catch squat. Oi finally asked him did he want some advice, and he said he guessed he could use it, so I told him if you wanna getcher wiener waxed ya gotta either gettum really young or really old, 'cause the women in the middle've got too much damn sense to fool around with people like him and me."

"What'd he say to that?"

"Not a damn thing. He just huffed and took off. Feller up to the post office told me come fall he moved back to Mass'chusetts."

6

The French Connection

Into the face of the young man who sat on the terrace of the Hotel Magnifique at Cannes there had crept a look of furtive shame, the shifty, hangdog look which announces that an Englishman is about to talk French.

—P. G. WODEHOUSE,
The Luck of the Bodkins

When you cross the mighty Restigouche River, turn right onto Québec Route 132, and head east down the Gaspé Peninsula toward Chaleur Bay, the landscape slowly changes, becoming softer, rounder, indefinably more sensuous than the monochromatically severe forestlands of northern New England and New Brunswick. And when you round the corner at St. Omer and head north-northeast along Baie de Cascapédia—past broad salt marshes, grand resort hotels, and gay seaside amusement parks; past lighthouse-tipped barrier peninsulas, trap-hauling lobsterboats, and shining seafood cafés garnished with umbrellas and seagulls; past smart boutiques with laughing long-legged shoppers, and broad sand beaches peppered with picnickers and well-basted nymphets crisping in the bright northern sun—you'd swear you had been mysteriously transported to Cape Cod or even, when you see the massive cathedrals that tower over every cozy seaside village, the South of France.

But when you look to your left and see the spruce-upholstered Chic-Choc Mountains that form all but the thin settled fringes of the Gaspé's unpeopled bosom, you know you're still in the north woods, albeit with a twist, for the Chic-Choc's soils are lushly sweet, not antiseptically sour, and the dozens of streams and rivers that spring from its pure heart flow clear as gems, free of the iced-tea tannin that stains standard-issue northwoods waterways.

In these diamond-and-emerald rivers swim sea trout and Atlantic salmon. And while it's true that here as elsewhere anadromous fish populations continue to wither beneath the corrosive forces of habitat destruction, overfishing, and regulatory timidity, it's also true that here as elsewhere the presence of even a few of these regal salmonids draws anglers from far and wide.

The remarkable thing about Québec is that so few of these anglers are Americans. Sometimes on New Brunswick's grand salmon rivers you can close your eyes, listen to the talk of fishing, and imagine yourself leaning against the counter at Manhattan's Urban Angler fly shop, while only a short drive away on the equally productive salmon rivers of Québec you'll hear only the rapid-fire incomprehensibility of the local brand of French. And when August rolls around and catch-and-release replaces the ten-fish season limit the Québecois too-generously award themselves, you won't even hear much of that, for catch-and-release is a new and suspicious concept in the land of *joie de vivre*. Of the crowds of salmon fishers that each year flock to the Gaspésie from Québec City and Montréal, few are willing to return home without, as a rueful river manager eyeing his threatened resource base told me, "a cooler filled with the trophies—these fine big fish I catch on my vacation and now give proudly to you, my neighbor and friend: *bon appétit.*"

American anglers, well accustomed to both catch-and-release and Puritan self-denial, are perfectly positioned to enjoy this seasonally neglected angling resource, yet few do. "I haven't parley voo'd since high school," they say, but that's a poor excuse. Of my high school French only bone-joor, o-vwah, mare-see, and joma-pell Jeem reliably survive, along with the vaguely musical memories that a place called Avignon has slippery bridges and some kinds of birds are unnecessarily jaunty. But in far less time than it took me to learn to tie a presentable dry fly, I puzzled out from a five-dollar French phrasebook that *138 Est* means "route 138 east," *172 Nord* means "route 172 north," a big red octagonal sign emblazoned with ARRÊTEZ means "stop," and that even if I can't pronounce them I can point to *ouefs* and *jambon* on a menu and smile, and the nice lady will bring me ham and eggs. And if I wiggle my fingers, she'll scramble them.

It's just as well to muzzle your high school French anyway, for the Québec article bears only passing resemblance to the Continental original taught in American schools. Years ago I stopped at a roadside convenience store to ask the way to the famous cathedral of Ste.-Anne-de-Beaupré, which two zealous young teachers of French meant to inflict on the busload of hypoglycemic high-schoolers I had chauffeured from midcoast Maine to Québec City. The French teachers tried out their haughtiest Parisian on the *dèppaneur*'s gas pump jockey but got for their efforts only blank stares, so I leaned out the school bus door and said, in my factory-equipment East Tennessee accent (which sounds, as a friend once so kindly pointed out, like Gomer Pyle after a botched root canal), "Par-DOAN miss you. Whar's 'at thar Cathy Drale Saint Andy Booper at soo voo play?" Suddenly he could speak better English than I do.

Although you wouldn't know it from the French-only signs that mark Québec's roads and shops and public edifices, almost everyone in Québec is schooled bilingually to some extent, and most will happily speak at least nominally comprehensible English once they understand you're merely a dumbass from the States mangling their language with the best of intentions and not an adamantly monolingual monarchist from Ottawa. Or, like the French teachers, putting on airs.

It's worth remembering, too, that America doesn't have the market cornered on nasty family squabbles that spill over into politics, as they had in that summer of impeachment fever. The French and the English, like many close cousins, have been at each other's throats for a millennium, calling a tense truce only in the past century to ally against a cyclical rash of Teutonic eruptions. But in America's multicultural neighbor to the north, the age-old war between the French and the English simmers on, with elements of the Québec French episodically threatening to separate from the Canadian confederation—freeing themselves from the English economic and cultural yoke, according to some, or hanging themselves and everyone else in Canada merely to spite the English, according to others.

If you're wondering what all this has to do with fishing, bear in mind that what little remains of North America's once enormous Atlantic salmon runs are divided between the nominally English Maritime Provinces and thoroughly French Québec. And the French and the English manage their fishing as differently as they manage their affairs of state, tables, and boudoirs.

If you like your salmon fishing on the English model, where fishing rights belong to but a privileged few, you need only phone for reservations at any number of splendidly exclusive Canadian salmon lodges and you can fish your beat, eat roast beef, and drink Scotch with people just like you. And don't forget to tip your guide, because it's against the law in New Brunswick for a nonresident to fish without one. But if you want your salmon fishing served up with ample helpings of *Liberté! Egalité! Fraternité!*—not to mention *pâte à choux,* a chilled Mâcon, and an elaborately impenetrable but decidedly small-*d* democratic system that provides, through a series of lottery drawings, unchaperoned time on the river for anyone willing to take a five-dollar chance on a sixty-dollar day ticket—you've got to storm that language barricade.

I'll buy an argument from a stateside salmon fisher who avoids exotic French Québec in favor of familiar English Canada because he can't abide food that hasn't been deep-fried then suffocated beneath a glutinous magma of canned beef gravy, but avoiding Québec because you don't speak French is simply a willful attempt to remain parochial.

"Most Americans don't even know this place exists," said Dave Bishop, sweeping his hand across the Petite Cascapédia's Home Pool. We were sitting at a picnic table in the dooryard of Camp Melançon near the covered-bridge hamlet of St. Edgar QC, watching the sun sink into this Gallatin-sized river that snakes down out of the wild Chic-Choc Mountains toward the glittering coast at New Richmond. Dave is a New Hampshire expatriate who spent his formative summers here with his Gaspesian mother and now runs a guide service in the area. I had watched him drop his canoe deftly through the pool while his Francophone sports laughed and talked and inexpertly fished the run, and had greeted him when he came ashore with my best nose-fluting bone-joor, to which he replied, in the compressed tones of northern New England, "Hey, howzit goin'?"

"There are fresh salmon in the river," he said, pointing out a nice fish rolling in a midstream lie. "More will come up when we get some rain, and fresh fish will keep coming into September. And there are sea trout, too, averaging maybe three pounds and going up to eight or nine. Most of the rod slots are filled now, but with the arrival of the catch-and-release season next month there'll be vacancies on all the rivers," he went on. "You'd think Americans would be all over this place."

I told Dave, an outfitter anxious to fill empty slots, that I thought they should be all over it, too, but I told myself, a temporary expatriate who had grown weary of his countrymen in that summer of twisted lies and bald-faced hypocrisy from both sides of the bipolar political world, that I was glad they weren't. At least not that week, anyway.

Half an hour later I was back on the coastal highway at an unpretentious little family-style restaurant Dave had recommended. For little more than the exchange-adjusted price of that international ambassador of American cuisine, le Beeg Mac and Frites, I dove headfirst into a great vat of cassoulet: white beans simmered together with tomatoes and sausage and lamb and goose confit and enough garlic to vaporize a vampire at a hundred yards. I filled chinks with chunks of crackling baguettes slathered with that lustrous ripe-cream butter found only in restaurants I can't afford and roadside beaneries in Québec. And then I had a piece of *tarte au sucre*—sugar pie, a thrombotic Gaspesian concoction of eggs and cream and butter and caramelized brown sugar quivering lasciviously in a crisp buttery shell.

For background music I had the animated chatter of fine young French families and their laughing children. Without knowing one word they said I understood all they were saying, or imagined I did, which is pretty much the same thing for a temporary expatriate grown weary of shrill family quarrels. I sat there beaming at the world like Balzac's Père Goriot, blissful in my uncomprehending ignorance, sipping coffee and listening to the sounds of happy laughter and wondering if I might actually die from another piece of pie, then deciding to find out. Of ignorance and delusion and feckless feasting is temporary happiness made.

The next morning I was back at the same table inhaling an airy omelet and talking with André Lepage, who with his big green canoe sitting just outside the window would be taking me for an overnighter down the Petite Cascapédia's remote East Branch, where an expressed interest in fishing someplace untrodden and wild and the luck of the draw at the Petite Cascapédia ZEC had sent me. These ZECs—Zone d'Exploitation Contrôlée, the local cooperatives that manage most Québec rivers—came into being in the nationalistic days of the 1970s, when French Canada's own violent family arguments led to, among other less pleasant things, miles of prime private water being pried lose from fat-cat owners and placed in public hands, a kind of salmon fishers' storming of the Bastille.

Each ZEC issues day-use permits by lottery, about half the winners being drawn on November 1 for the following season and the other half being held for day-ticket drawings at the ZEC's office. In other words, everyone, rich or poor alike, gets an equal chance at one of the good spots. *Vive l'Egalité!* Or at least temporarily so, for rumors of ZECs selling plum blocks of river time to outfitters were just then beginning to stir. Privilege and money have long greedy fingers, and small-*d* democracies possessing anything of value are everywhere besieged. So it's *Vive l'Egalité*, kind of, at least for a while, as the endless cyclicity of family squabbles plays itself out: Who gets the tough-tendoned drumstick and who the tender breast? Who gets Grannie's Queen Anne highboy and who her leftover suppositories? Who gets the good fishing and who the bad? Guess.

After breakfast we drove some forty kilometers into the Chic-Chocs, steadily climbing snaky logging roads through a Crown land forest of thick spruce and fir. Finally we came to our put-in on the

East Branch—up here little more than a wade-across trout stream, with stair-step rapids soughing into broad, gravel-bottomed pools and water so cold it numbed the hands even in the first week of July. "We first to go down ze East Branch thees year," André said, testing the water. "But could be we are too err-lee." Last winter brought almost no snow here, he explained, and the spring rains that flooded New England crowded south of the Gaspé, leaving the peninsula's rivers low, cold, and supernaturally clear—good for the fish, André thought, though not so good for the fishing. Still, he remained relentlessly optimistic through what turned out to be a taxing twelve-hour day. "Around the next bend," he'd say as we corkscrewed through the river's compact canyons, which funneled into our faces a building and persistently contrary wind. "Past the next falls," he'd be certain as he leaned into his setting pole and eased the heavy canoe down through another set of bony rapids, beaching it alongside yet another picture-book pool that promised much and delivered little, at least in tangible terms.

At one faceted emerald pool with a swirling back eddy deep enough to hide a loaded log truck, André hauled out a little plastic periscope and spotted a couple of salmon in the fifteen-pound range holding tight against the bottom. Although I had suspected fish in the other pools, this time I knew not only that fish awaited but also their exact sizes and locations, this from peeping down at them like an upside-down submariner plotting a spread shot on a pair of tankers. But after unsuccessfully drifting a virtual fly shop past their lie, I decided that imagining a fish might lie here or there and that with the right drift or the right fly the fish might briefly be mine was far preferable to knowing a fish lay precisely there and realizing I was being pointedly ignored.

As plunge pools gave way to slow runs and we entered prime sea trout country, I slammed big streamers toward the bank—under, beside, and into overhanging trees, taking fourteen-inch brook trout now and then and losing flies just as often, along with three fine sea trout that wrapped me in the roots, their broad speckled tails placing them well into the five-pound range. "Trouts tight against ze bank," André said. "If you doan hang up now and then in ze trees you are not cas-teeng close enough." I'm always eager to follow a guide's instructions when they agree with my preconceived notions, and so I erred on the generous side of now and then hanging up in the trees. Once, as my huge bucktail spun around a limb, hung briefly in midair, then slid slowly to the water, a long black torpedo shot out from beneath the bank and slammed it back into the tree, like a barracuda chasing a needlefish into the mangroves. "*Beeg* trouts," said André. "Cast again, queek queek," but with my fly woven tightly into the tree's warp and woof there could be no quick follow-up cast, not with that fly or for that matter to that fish, doubtless still laughing about my frantic efforts to free the line.

That evening we camped on the gravel bar where the East and West Branches join to form the Petite Cascapédia. As we crouched over a driftwood fire wolfing down huge slabs of his forty-sixth birthday cake and smoking away the mosquitoes and no-see-ums that stabbed exposed flesh like irate little soldering irons, André admitted that, with the cold low water and the resulting late runs of fish, we might well have done better downriver near the camp, unfished water or not. But as the river played its tunes, and the mists swirled through these scale-model Alps, and the night closed in silent and lonely and blissfully wild while not fifteen miles was the closest thing in North America to the Côte d'Azur, I could think of nowhere else on earth I'd rather be, fish or no fish. Not that there had been no fish. Had I been home in Maine, all those fourteen-inch brook trout would have made for a grand day of fishing, one I'd remember for years. Measured against the yardstick of twenty-pound salmon and eight-pound sea trout, however, they had seemed merely distractions. Thomas Berger might have been thinking of fly fishing when he wrote in *Little Big Man* that all unhappiness comes from having standards.

The next day dawned to a chill steady rain, and we lingered long over coffee and thick dripping sandwiches made from homemade pork pâté and strawberry jam before finally loading up and shoving off down the main river. We had floated seventeen kilometers yesterday and had another ten to go before the takeout.

This sector was all Atlantic salmon water, with enormous slow pools that had produced fish to thirty pounds last year, but although we saw fish here and there I still couldn't get them to take in the ice-clear water. Mostly they crouched barely visible in bedrock seams at the bottoms of deep, deep pools, refusing even to glance at the flies I drifted by their noses—a magnificent indifference that is, I suppose, the divine right of the fish of kings.

I spent the next night only a half hour's drive away yet in a vastly different world: Château Blanc, a modest oceanfront hotel in the bustling resort town of Bonaventure, where instead of mist-lapped mountains veiled by wood smoke and mist and mosquitoes I had as scenery a big C&C sloop skirting the shore. As it tacked, its big maple-leaf foresail crackling like gunfire, it scattered flotillas of cormorants and seals—those hungry protected predators that wait at the mouths of rivers for young salmon heading off to sea. Those who survive this openmouthed gauntlet will grow big and strong and return to this very river to spawn, at least those that aren't netted off Greenland and sold for three dollars a pound.

As the sporadic showers of the past few days thickened into a full-blown rainstorm, I drove a half mile to *très* upscale Camp Bonaventure, where I visited briefly with manager Glenn LeGrand, a friend of a friend, and exchanged brief generic pleasantries with moneyed American guests anxious that I know where they had fished and with whom. Just as the first Bill and Monica jokes were about to begin, my guide Mario Poirier arrived, and we escaped for an evening on the big Bonaventure and a different breed of salmon fishing.

We headed for an unlimited-access pool a few miles from town, where the bright lights and festival atmosphere of the riverside cottages and campers contrasted sharply with the East Branch of the Petite Cascapédia's wild solitude. Of course the Bonaventure has equally wild stretches farther up into the Chic-Chocs, but you have to be luckier in the draw than I was. Still, who was I to complain? My lottery drawing on the East Branch had sent me down unfished wilderness water; it was only fitting that my next river on this loose dice-shaking itinerary should send me into the public fray.

Several dozen wading anglers and a dozen or more boats surrounded the big pool, everyone fishing methodically downstream in the regulation manner—three good casts then four steps down for the waders; a dozen sequentially lengthened casts then a ten-foot drop off the anchor for the boats. And then the next hopeful angler would work in from above, everyone talking back and forth and laughing and enjoying their lives, children playing, women singing, lanterns hissing, the smell of Coleman fuel, smoldering charcoal, and searing meat heavy in the air. No one caught anything, but no one really seemed to care, possessed as they were by the warm glow of *Fraternité!* and the ineffable optimism of fly anglers trying to gull the ultimate enigma: a fish that doesn't feed in fresh water.

I figured the fishers must greatly outnumber the fish in this transient riverside city, but between puffs of Captain Black and pointed comments about prissy tapered leaders versus a simple and infallible nine-foot hunk of fifteen-pound-test Maxima, Mario said as many as a hundred salmon might be holding in that pool—one of the river's best, he said. And he should know, he added with a touch of chest-thumping Gallic pride, for he grew up on this river and has guided here since leaving the Royal Canadian Air Force eight years past, and his father guided here for forty-five years before him. This stretch of water, he said, is always full of fish. On conformational cue, a twenty-pound salmon leapt straight up not thirty feet from the canoe and fell back with a great kerwhacking splash, and as the evening progressed a half dozen fish of various sizes cleared the surface within our skirmish line—keeping tabs, perhaps, on the regimented activities of this air-breathing army intent on striking their jaws with steel, knocking them on the head, filling their cavities with shallots and thyme, and laying them tenderly across one of the waiting Webers that lofted smoke signals over the pool like Hollywood Indians tracking the Seventh Cavalry.

Mario was right about the pool being full of fish. He was right about my prissy tapered leader, too, as I found when I replaced it with an honest hunk of level Maxima and my line control improved tenfold. What he was wrong about was thinking the Black Bear, or the Cosseboom, or the Butterfly, or the Green Machine, or the Black Dose, or the Magog Smelt, or any of the other fanciful confections I kept tying hopefully to the end of that leader might tempt one of those closemouthed salmon into striking—salmon that, with the prevailing low water, had likely been sulking in the river for weeks and had seen every fly known to humankind. Perhaps more than any other fish, the Atlantic salmon frustrates its would-be harassers with its taciturn unpredictability. And this is the root of its attraction. What is easily attained is as easily forgotten, and what is won by long perseverance is ever remembered. Or so goes the theory.

Frankly, after an evening of unrequited casting to intermittently visible fish I would have been happy to forgo hoary traditions and sportsmanlike eyewash and blast one of those leaping buggers at the peak of his hang time with a load of buckshot. When taunted, East Tennesseeans turn mean.

The next day was Canada Day, a confederational celebration akin to the U.S. Fourth of July, only less commemorative, as you can appreciate, of ancestral abilities to punch .54-caliber holes in Red Tunics. As I got ready to head east for the next leg of this semistructured journey, the hotel's parking lot quickly began filling with celebrants from Québec City and Montréal, a striking number of their cars laden with equal measures of beach-play paraphernalia and salmon rods. I didn't see one vehicle that clearly belonged to the dedicated species of gimlet-eyed FisherMan so common in American and New Brunswick fishing towns—the giant SUVs with big tires and mirrored windows and a king's ransom of fishing tackle, vehicles that carry Men to Battle, not families to play. And it was then that I began to understand how central to the Québec family psyche the Atlantic salmon actually is. Here it is not just a fish, as it is in English Canada—albeit the king of fish and an economic cornerstone in salmon-river country. Nor is it a ghostly remnant on its bureaucratically bungled way into oblivion, as it is in the States. In Québec the Atlantic salmon is a societal totem, a unifying symbol of nationalistic desire not unlike the American bald eagle, if bald eagles were hunted down and trussed up and laid out on smoking grills with their abdominal cavities stuffed with shallots and thyme. Atlantic salmon would have far better chances of surviving a polluted, hungry, and exponentially overpopulated world if they weren't so damn tasty to a whole host of predators, from seals and shags and Greenland gillnetters to lip-smacking epicures with a fly rod in one hand and a basting brush in the other.

There's no denying the lure of Atlantic salmon, on both a sporting and a culinary level: the complexity and delicious uncertainty of catching them; the way they strike a fly for no definable reason, then leap like Masai warriors and peel line off the reel so fast it screams like a cat with its tail in a blender; the way they return to their natal rivers to perpetuate their species, then return to the sea to feed and roam before returning again and again and not, like Pacific salmon, swim home and get their ashes hauled once then turn belly-up and croak; the way their flesh yields resiliently to a gentle finger when it reaches that magic moment between too rare and perfectly pink, just before it begins to flake. When I think of Atlantic salmon it's hard to think of fly rods straining in wild beautiful places without also thinking of clarified butter sizzling in the sauté pan while lemon zest and capers and a dusty bottle of overpriced Meursault wait expectantly on the sideboard.

But with runs dwindling worldwide, when I think of fishing for Atlantic salmon I think increasingly of necrophilia. Such is its fascination that I do it anyway—Atlantic salmon fishing I mean—at least on those rare occasions when I can afford this sport of royalty, or can manufacture an excuse to write a magazine article about it and so justify (and deduct) the sobering cost. Meanwhile I quell culinary longings with farm-raised salmon then lean back in my chair and pick my teeth with a rib bone, polishing off the six-dollar supermarket Chardonnay and glowing with self-righteousness about preserving the wild resource. At least that's what I did before learning that farm-raised salmon often escape to spread exotic diseases and undesirable genes along with their milt and eggs sown carefree in the wild.

There is no escaping guilt in this complex world. There is only measuring it by your own moral yardstick and hoping for the best, unless you're a politician and can live by loading your own guilt onto someone else.

Beyond Bonaventure the broad sand beaches gradually give way to sheer surf-pounded cliffs of brick-red sandstone. Cape Cod and the

French Riviera slowly morph into Big Sur and the Oregon coast, while the Gaspé's pop-bead chain of glossy tourist-tweaking towns becomes a sparse sprinkle of modest mouse-hole fishing villages, with small trim houses peeking from behind mountains of lobster traps and fish-drying flakes, and the ever-present Catholic churches becoming smaller and more rustic but no less central and dominating. The road winds and climbs and plunges and twists like an electrocuted nightcrawler, and if I'd had a Lotus instead of a four-cylinder Toyota with a half ton of slide-in camper in the bed and a hundred thousand miles on the odometer it would have been an exhilarating drive, with all the heeling and toeing and sawing at the gearbox to the sexy whir of redlining camshafts and ejaculating fuel injectors as a body could stand. But even in my faithful old wheezing Toyota it was a gorgeous drive, or at least what I could see of it was, when I could pry my eyes from the twisting narrow road and the mad-hatter French drivers and the five-hundred-foot plummet to the crashing waves below.

At Percé—a land's-end enclave of touristy kitsch complete with wizened Olde Salts sporting yellow slickers and Popeye pipes who hawk lobster-trap ashtrays and lighthouse saltshakers to vacationing urbanites in cable-knit sweaters and new Greek fishermen's caps—the peninsula turns sharply north and becomes even more alpinesque, and shortly thereafter the corrugated land quickly smooths and the road spirals down to a broad enveloped plain, where the bay and town of Gaspé come into view. In 1534 Jacques Cartier planted a cross here to mark his new water route to China. Since, like all the other trans–North American water routes to China, this one petered out in frowning forests and unnavigable rapids, the cross now marks only the happy confluence of the York, Dartmouth, and St.-Jean Rivers—three very different bodies of water, and far more important in the grand scheme of things than a quick route to

China, at least if you fish for salmon, as nearly everyone in Québec seems to do.

The luck of the draw and its protected exclusivity kept me off the St.-Jean, but ZEC manager Don Bourgouin, another friend of a friend in the tiny insular world of Atlantic salmon fishing, took me on a whirl-wind tour of this wild little river where he grew up playing and now manages. The St.-Jean belongs among the world's great beauty spots: isolated and wild as a bear, a majestic crystal cascade bounding sym-phonically through soaring forests as untouched as can be traversed in a bouncing, wheel-spinning pickup truck. Of course to anglers beauty is more than scenery-deep: I watched five great salmon finning quietly in the transparent depths of Big Indian Pool, and angler success rates on the St.-Jean are among the highest in Canada. Still, you can enter the ZEC's lottery and have just as much chance at one of the St.-Jean's limited spots as anyone else. And if you've done well in the game of life and would rather eliminate the uncertainty, you can always pop $700 Canadian a day ($450 after August 10 and catch-and-release season ar-rives) for a stay at the exclusive Pavilion lodge and its own private water.

Personal economics and the luck of the permit draw put me on the Dartmouth, a fine little river suffering, the day I was there, from too much rain falling too fast after too much drought. Still, after finding a pool upstream of the muddy runoff from a logging opera-tion on the Dartmouth's western flank, I got a couple of what salmon fishers call "nice pulls." In the increasing uncertainty—some would say futility—that characterizes Atlantic salmon fishing in this dawn of a hungry new century, a couple of nice pulls is enough to make your day. It pretty much has to be.

The next day I doubled the cape and headed west along the Gaspé's rugged St. Lawrence shore, where the Chic-Chocs crowd down to the sea and the thinly scattered fishing villages notch deeply into granite. I spent that night near the town of Petite-Vallée at Pourvoirie Beauséjour, a prime example of a peculiarly French institution unknown in America: a cushy family-oriented inn crossed with a catch-your-own-fish market built on a silent mirrored pond with, as a sign said, a limit of 15 TRUITT per day. Fishing from an electric-propelled floating cement trough for an hour or so before dinner, I released (surreptitiously, catch-and-release being positively forbidden, according to another sign and an imperious fish warden) a baker's dozen of fat brook trout that rose to a sporadic hex hatch. I felt, with my lovely old cane rod and long fine leader, quite the seasoned angler, until I saw that the eight-year-olds on shore had done just as well slinging red-and-white spoons with Mickey Mouse–edition Zebcos. It was like fishing in a hatchery, really. Massive underground springs feed the pond, which is by eastern standards significantly alkaline; the stocked brookies that splashed everywhere grew fat as Poland Chinas on the inexhaustible invertebrate banquet that flourished in the icy nutriment roux.

It isn't the kind of place frequented by the modern American fly fisher—a hatch-matching absolutist who would sooner kill his mother than a trout. Of course trout fishing isn't the main attraction at "fish camps" like Pourvoirie Beauséjour but more of an added fillip to the meals, the relaxation, the *Fraternité*. Still, everyone from Grandma to grandkids fished when I was there, and everyone took home a cooler full of trout. Which is as it should be in a heavily stocked pond literally boiling with forage in a land in love with its collective stomach.

It's easy to forget, in these intolerant times, that trout are a renewable resource, just as salmon were before environmental degradation and rampant commercial fishing put them on life support.

Although it can be a hard message to get across, trout as a species are far less fragile than salmon. A few years ago I was having dinner at a Denver restaurant with a tableful of evangelical fly-fishing enthusiasts brought together by the Fly Tackle Dealer Show, and the subject wandered around to catch-and-release. My argument that catch-and-release is a management tool with roots more economic than ethical fell on deaf ears with this crowd, and when I chose rainbow trout from the menu you would think I had turned cannibal—this despite the menu's claim that these trout grew up on a farm in Idaho. They looked on in disgust as I slid a fork down the backbone and peeled off a boneless fillet, then lifted out the skeleton by the head, pried out the buttery little cheek muscles with my fingernail, and popped them into my mouth.

The meal passed in disapproval and frosty silence. I didn't bother to defend my practice of eating trout now and then—even wild ones—because I thought it would be more fun to do it at a later date in a more public forum, when I could point out that three of the most horrified had been eating that night's special: swordfish, snatched from a decimated and dwindling gene pool by a miles-long line bristling with thousands of hooks that indiscriminately kill anything big enough to cram the bait in its mouth. I'd love to mention their names—you'd recognize them all—but that would be in bad taste. And doubtless actionable.

For all its *Fraternité*, Pourvoirie Beauséjour was the first place on the Gaspé I felt out of place. Here for the first time I sat down with people not united by the universal glue of fly fishing, which makes temporary compatriots of Frenchmen and Englishmen in the same way a shared interest in smoking and a limited number of smoking facilities might make companions of CEOs and janitors. And this far from the cities, the other guests' high school English had survived no better than my high school French. But finally a friendly young couple with a usable vestige of English, a budding interest in fly fishing, and an extra helping of compassion for a hapless foreigner took me under their wing, helping me navigate the menu and later whisking me away to a mountaintop pavilion to watch the sun set over the pinkening St. Lawrence. We talked into the night, in our halting awkward mixture of broken French and English and pantomime, about how the world was and how we wished it were, how we hoped someday to find someone to vote for and not merely someone to vote against. As we parted back at the lodge Paulette said, "You are easy to speak the English with. You are speaking it just like we do." I wasn't sure what this meant but I took it as a compliment, or at least I did until I called my wife the next day and she asked why I was talking like Pepe LePew, the cartoon skunk.

West from Petite-Vallée the country becomes increasingly rugged and the road steeper and more sinuous as it tries to carve its way into the sheer shoulders of the Chic-Chocs, until just past the ZEC office at the Rivière-la-Madeleine it abandons the attempt altogether and cantilevers over the St. Lawrence on concrete piers.

By St.-Anne-des-Monts the Chic-Chocs begin their retreat from the coast into the distant heights of the Gaspésie Provincial Park, and by the town of Matane the Gaspé becomes broad rolling farmland, its prosperous modern towns cut with roadside picnic grounds that fill at noon with families and coolers and baskets groaning with sandwiches and salads and the inevitable bottle of wine.

By dawdling en route I had missed my ferry at Matane, and as I waited for the next I went into town to look at the river, a popular spot for American anglers, at least in its upper reaches, and for Québecois anglers from all around the province. Downtown Matane literally wraps itself around salmon. At lunchtime everyone heads for the promenade to watch anglers climb down steep aluminum ladders to the river below the dam. If someone hooks a fish, the crowd erupts with cheers and laughter and applause.

The town park is built around the fish ladder. Vacationers come bedecked with cameras and curiosity; lovers stroll hand in hand and gaze into the water; excited schoolchildren, beaming grandmothers, pierced scowling teens with eggplant-colored hair—all come to peer into the fish ladder hoping for a glimpse of *le saumon*. One and all eagerly cough up their Twoonies—the two-dollar Canadian coin—for a trip downstairs to the viewing ports, where they cluster around the glass windows cut into the fish ladder's side and look at the resting salmon with a tender love that's embarrassing for a tight-assed American cynic to behold.

Six salmon held in the resting pools: three grilse of five to seven pounds, a pair of fifteen-pound hens, and a big ugly jaw-jutting male crowding thirty-five pounds. Old men and boys pressed against the glass excitedly, pointing and laughing and Mon Dieuing like Inspector Clouseau. A pair of giggling adorable teenyboppers in braids and parochial school uniforms formed perfect Os of astonishment with their gum-popping mouths as the big cockfish flexed his muscles and sent an intruding grilse spiraling off into the current.

La Belle Province's educational efforts seem to be instilling a populationwide reverence for salmon—and by extension for the pure environment that sustains both their species and ours—and are doing so far more successfully than the American educational establishment's warm and fuzzy Disneyland approach, where nothing ever dies and humans stand apart from the environment. Kids, adults should remember but never seem to, are smart and critical, and have highly developed bullshit detectors. No wonder Generations X and Y don't bother to vote. Who would such media-savvy creatures vote for?

That afternoon I rode the ferry some forty miles across and down the broad St. Lawrence to industrially malignant Baie-Comeau, with its smoking factories and mines and dark satanic mills, its shining new

Wal-Marts and McDonald'ses and KFCs sprouting from raw corporate chasms freshly gnawed into the forest, then I drove some 130
miles down the almost unpopulated and spectacularly wild North
Shore. This is quintessential north woods: vast expanses of Precam-
brian granite thinly smeared with stunted black spruce and sour peat
cut with tannin-stained rivers and brawling waterfalls that in more
marketable regions would be obscured by crowds of admiring
tourists but are here seen only by the drivers of log trucks and occasional wanderers searching out the unknown.

At every river I wanted to stop, uncase my rod, shoulder a backpack, and trek off into the untrekked, but it was going dark, and in
muskeg country an incautious step can easily be your last. And theoretically I was supposed to be at this very moment checking into a
salmon lodge way west of here, writing a magazine article that was
the ostensible purpose behind my semistructured wandering. But I
had missed my ferry by dawdling and thought that this might provide
sufficient cover for dawdling some more, and finally I saw a grown-
over two-track crawling up a riverbank, nosed up it, and parked in an
old log yard overlooking a silent black river left unnamed on my
highway map. I felt my way to the shore, fly rod in hand, and as the
mosquitoes and no-see-ums argued over first claim I caught two small
trout on a big Hornberg twitched dry across a slow black eddy. I
cleaned them in the stream and flung their innards into the bushes,
then I fried them quickly in good Québec butter. I sliced an apple
and a crusty *bâtard* I'd bought at a *dèppaneur*, and sat there eating by
candlelight, watching phoebes hover outside the screens picking off
mosquitoes and listening to a concert of fluting peepers and *farump-
ing* frogs underlain by the treble trickle of black water on stone and
the low-brass rumble of distant log trucks on pavement and the occasional *wooowah* of riverine traffic warding off the fog. I could have
stayed forever.

Still, the next morning I headed on westward to do my job, and near ancient Tadoussac, a thriving trading post when Champlain arrived in 1603 now gone to sandal making, T-shirt selling, and whale-watching for its daily bread, I turned up the valley of the Saguenay River and then its tributary the Ste.-Marguerite.

Only a few hours' drive from Québec City, and with Route 172 running along much of its length, the Ste.-Marguerite is more urbane than wilderness rivers like the St.-Jean, although its demi-Yosemite setting is fully as splendid, with miniature Half Domes looming around every bend. And it has the major advantage, for the gastronomically inclined, of a four-star restaurant perched right on its banks at Hôtellerie Bardsville, my roundabout destination.

Where I had expected to meet imperious marketing majors anxious to push their fishing facilities onto the charge cards of American anglers through the medium of an outdoor-writer invitation, I met instead a perceptive and flashingly intelligent Chantal Grenier, the Ste.-Marguerite River Association manager, and her boyfriend Patrick Corbeil, a whale researcher and recent demon convert to fly fishing who was, Chantal said, to be my new best friend, at least for the next few days. We spent hours that evening talking and laughing and getting to know one another, all the while snarfling our way through smoked duck breast, and sautéed trout stuffed with wild mushrooms and scallops, and poached pears sleekly gilded with chocolate and crème Anglaise, maintaining our increasingly sluggish circulation with a couple of bottles of medicinal beverages. As Chantal's happy guest I had no need to fumble for my own charge card, but I couldn't help but eye the menu and make some rough exchange-rate calculations: At sixty cents American to the Canadian dollar, three of us ate like potentates for about what the nightly synthetic special would have cost us at the Olive Garden or Applebee's or any of the other aggressive chain-drive restaurants that homogenize our national tastes.

Sooner or later, however, you have to shove away from the table and rig your rod, even in Québec, and the Ste.-Marguerite, like the rivers of the Gaspé, was low and clear and demanding. The next morning I moved a nice fish at the *observatoire* pool near the hotel, where a big wooden deck jutting over the river provides a platform for guests and hotel staff to enjoy their morning coffee and croissants while commenting on your casting style, but I think the salmon was merely amusing himself at my expense and had no intention of taking a double Green Machine in classic dry-fly water, at least not where people could see him. Perhaps he was astonished even to be shown such a thing.

The elaborate food served at Hôtellerie Bardsville is in line with the elaborate paraphernalia of Atlantic salmon fishing itself. Sometimes when I open my fly book and gaze at its garish contents, I feel I should don smoked glasses to protect my eyes. I know perfectly well I could fish a simple basic-black wet fly with a flounce of fluorescent green floss circling its butt and catch roughly as many salmon as I would if I tried every confection that centuries of feverish fisherminds have devised, but what fun would that be? A fish caught so infrequently must be surrounded by elaborate rituals if it's to hold our interest.

Patrick and I fished hard all that day and the next through intermittent showers, or perhaps more accurately showers of intermittent velocity, for it never stopped raining that I could see. Yet with all the rain the river never rose an inch, a testament to the absorbency of the surrounding countryside now that a new provincial park prevents its wholesale conversion into toilet paper. We saw lots of beautiful water and lots of beautiful, blasé salmon, Patrick and I, but neither of us stuck one. In my defense I did catch five members of the salmonid family, though their combined lengths didn't quite equal the twenty-five inches that defines a legal salmon in Québec.

With the low water bringing in few new salmon from the sea, and with what fish there were having grown bored with anglers over the crowded St.-Jean-Baptiste and Canada Day holidays, a change of venue seemed in order, so the next day we climbed aboard nasty snarling little ATVs—Patrick behind Chantal, me behind Yvon-Marie Gauthier, the ZEC's Chief Guardian and an old-guard northwoods trapper and guide with thirty-five years on the river whom, in his feathered slouch hat, you could easily imagine singing "Alouette" while paddling up an unexplored river to marry a Montangais—and we bounced off up the steep muddy trail for the Murrailles Branch, a beautifully remote little tributary that had seen no anglers thus far this season.

Riding one of those infernal machines was a novel experience for an inveterate walker like me. I was afraid, like the died-in-the-spinnaker sailor who went cruising on a powerboat, that I might find it enjoyable, but instead I merely found it convenient, shortening to fifteen minutes a one-hour hike and thereby extending our fishing time at the expense of my environmental self-righteousness. I still would rather have walked and enjoyed the scenery and the silence and the freedom from puffing hydrocarbons, but I couldn't very well impose my views on others, as un-American as that sounds.

We ate a quick lunch at the ZEC's tiny four-person outpost cabin nestled into a pizza-shaped clearing in the unbroken forest, then, with Yvon-Marie and his chain saw in the lead, we headed for the camp pool, slashing our way through the winter's fresh crop of blowdowns. Last year, Patrick said, he had seen eighty salmon holding in this pool. In this dry year there were only three, but one crowded thirty pounds and none looked jaded.

As guest and visiting writer I should have fished first, but Chantal, on a rare trip out of the office, was so enthusiastic and bubbling and looked so much like Juliette Binoche in *The Unbearable Lightness of Being* that I insisted she go ahead of me—a good thing, because

Yvon-Marie, who like Patrick and me was thoroughly mad about enchanting Chantal and who, moreover, was armed with a chain saw, clearly intended that she get first crack, visiting writer or not.

So Chantal waded in while I climbed the opposite bluff to spot and, I hoped, take photographs for the article I was theoretically here to write. As her fly swung its way downstream two of the fish evaporated in that spooky sine-wave way fish have of disappearing, but one stood his ground and twitched like a flea-bit dog every time the Colburn Special passed his nose. I showed Chantal with my hands how far she must lengthen her line to get the fly literally in his face and hopefully antagonize him into striking. Finally after the fly's third obtrusive trip past his snout he'd had enough, and he chased it into the shallows and murthered it nearly at Chantal's feet. And, as they say, the battle was joined.

The salmon was not happy and showed it in the usual theatrical fashion, but Chantal was as happy as a human can legally be and wasn't shy about expressing it. What came echoing through the forest is a bit hard to describe—like one of those Wagnerian operas where a large German woman is slowly disemboweled by a butter knife, only louder and more bloodcurdling. I wondered, as she whooped and squealed and shrieked and screamed, whether lovely, excited, and ecstatically happy Chantal might make noises like these when . . . Oh. Excuse me. Forget I said that. Bad writer. *Naughty* writer.

Finally Chantal brought the fish to net and fussed over it with the tender solicitude of a new mother, worried her fifteen minutes of warfare had injured this precious returnee to the river she relentlessly parents: last night at dinner she had railed loudly and bitterly about the *viandeaux*—meat fishermen—who take her salmon home to stuff with shallots and thyme. Then the salmon slapped his tail and sped into the pool, and we all sat down and smiled and laughed and unplugged our ears.

As it happened, Chantal's fifteen-pounder was the only fish of the day, but we were all gallantly happy for her and didn't feel a bit sorry for ourselves. Honest.

The next day's newspaper brought ugly news: Although I can read but few words of French I could read the date, and in two days, I realized with a shock, I had magazine page proofs to review. It was time to head for home.

Although my road trip through Québec did nothing to boost my lifetime Atlantic salmon count past sixteen or, despite my best efforts, my waist size past thirty-three, I was happy to discover I could drive twelve hundred miles through splendid fishing country at the height of summer in a readily accessible country whose dollar is worth sixty-two cents and see exactly five American license plates, and never once, as far as I could tell, suffer through a joke about the inappropriate deployment of cigars or the definition of *is*. When it comes to language barriers, *Vive la différence.*

7

Disappointing Carlos

I find that if men at this day would vanquish their passions, and free themselves from the snares of covetousnesse, leaving many fruitlesse and pernicious designes, without doubt they might live at the Indies very pleasant and happily: for that which other Poets sing of the Elisean fields & of the famous Tempe, or that which Plato reports or feignes of his Atlantike Iland; men should find in these Lands, if with a generous spirit they would choose rather to command their silver and their desires, then to remain to it slaves as they are . . . [but] There are some windes which blow . . . and are, as it were, Lords thereof, not admitting any entrie or communication of their contraries.

—JOSEPH ACOSTA,
The Naturall Historie of the West Indies

"*Y*ou are not seeing good the fish," Carlos said, shaking his head as wearily as though I were some sad scion of his loins spending my days slumped before the television and my nights carousing in bars.

"*Fish?* Where?" I asked, sighting down the line of his outstretched arm.

"There! There! Ten o'clock! Fifty feet!" he said, jabbing with his finger.

"Right. I got 'em," though of course I was lying. I just didn't want to disappoint Carlos, who is, after all, the patriarch of fly-fishing guides on Ambergris Cay, or so everyone says.

So I launched a cast toward what looked like where he was pointing and what I guessed was about fifty feet, and because the wind was gusting upward of twenty knots I punched in a little extra oomph—and, of course, the wind chose just that moment to pause for breath and the fly splatted the water like a belly-flopping albatross. The bonefish, needless to say, flushed like quail. I had no trouble seeing that.

I looked astern, where Carlos shook his head sadly. "You got to learn to see them," he said. "And maybe work a bit on your casting."

"I'll get it," I said, though I don't think either of us actually believed this.

There is nothing so pathetic as a small-stream trout specialist on a tough bonefish flat. All the studied responses of a lifetime are suddenly useless—no, more than useless: They are implacable impediments. On the flats things must happen instantly, but years of oozing up sylvan brooks like a sedated heron, spying out amorphous trout shimmering ephemerally in liquid crystal and sitting down to take their measure before methodically crafting a close approach had made me a plodding slow coach of an angler adrift in a land of cast-cast-now-now. And along with my ingrained inertia I was also regretting, as I looked to my wrist for navigational guidance and saw only WE 7–14—1:39.12P, the day I ever bought a digital watch.

"Nervous water! Nervous water! Twelve o'clock!" Carlos kept saying, but in the violent puffs of wind the water at ten, two, and four looked equally nervous to me. "Mud! Mud! Three o'clock!" he said again and again, but as I conjured a clock face and scanned the cardinal points for the mud slicks of bonefish rooting for shrimp and crabs, I saw nothing but mud. Miles of mud.

Previous flats trips had spoiled me: bright sunny skies, soft tropical breezes, hard sandy bottoms, ice-clear water—soft conditions that left plenty of time for even me to react. But here in Belize, where behind the world's second longest barrier reef two hundred square miles of fishable flats endlessly absorb nutrient soup from the well-watered mainland, the bottom is in many places not sand but sticky knee deep ooze. And then there was that tight-spinning low that sprawled like a great orange hydra across the Weather Channel printout posted in the lodge's office window, a low that was busily beating all that skinny transparent water and bottomless ooze into an opaque latte froth.

If I was not seeing good the fish it was for a good reason. At least that's what I kept saying, by way of explaining my sorry actions to a disappointed Carlos and to an even more disappointed me. And we weren't really after bonefish anyway but tarpon, I kept reminding myself, for July is when the big tarpon crowd onto the Belizean flats looking for action, in the best singles-bar sense of the word. But with the enormous spiraling low peering over our shoulders even Carlos couldn't see the tarpon. Combine that with my medicated Mister Magoo tactics and I had no more chance of getting some action than if I had swaggered into a Goth bar wearing a lime-green leisure suit and singing Barry Manilow.

෨   ෨   ෨   ෨   ෨   ෨

We had started the day hunting tarpon along the expansive flats around Savannah Cay, some twenty miles west of the Ambergris Cay town of San Pedro. When we left El Pescador Lodge it was sunny, with a light breeze that smelled of bougainvillea and raw sugar, but a hard black line underscored the sun as it slipped like an incandescent orange from the blue eastern seas, and by the time we reached Savannah the wind was piping past twenty knots, the Absolut sea had turned the color of the owl and the pussycat's boat, and the sky was the color of a flat tire.

"De weather too bad," Carlos finally had said, peering through the gloom and leaning on his gnarled ironwood pole like a Mayan mystic lifted from a carving at Tikal. "Can no see tarpons in this. Maybe better we go catch some bonefish. Always we catch the bonefish." So we pounded back toward San Pedro and ducked into the lee of the mangroves around Cayo Cangrejo, where Carlos quickly began spotting bonefish and I quickly did not.

In days to come I got to where I could spot them, at least some of the time. Either that or I got to where I could pretend I'd spotted them and drop a fly fifty feet out at ten o'clock in the unpredictable gusts, sometimes even hitting where I had pretended to be aiming. Often the bonefish were pretty hard to miss, even for me, because they traveled the flats not as ghostly ones and twos but in schools more accurately described as wads—great boiling brown knots of fish that rolled up and down the flats like tumbleweeds. When I could keep them in sight through the gray gloom and vector a cast into their capricious paths through the stiff random puffs, a fine flashing bone would pounce on the fly like a miniature jaguar. And if I could maneuver it through the gauntlet of snapping barracudas and embryonic mangroves spiking up from the mud like the fingers of drowning sailors reaching out for a monofilament lifeline, and bring it boatside and ease the Gotcha from its jaw, then I would get to watch it speed wildly away, like a chrome-plated sucker hopped up on amphetamines. I could nurture a small sense of accomplishment at this. And I could feel that maybe, for a change, I had not disappointed Carlos.

And this was not such a bad goal to have. We had gotten to know each other pretty well, Carlos and I. In the mornings we would hunt tarpon, drifting at the edge of the deep waters just off Cangrejo, where the big tarpon sweep onto the flats in ones and twos. And in the afternoons, when the daily squalls drifted in with the tide from the storm lingering to the east and clouded the visibility all hunters need, we would go after bonefish, often having cracks at hundreds at a time. And sometimes we would hunt permit, though always unsuccessfully, always seeing them too late or too far upwind to pole within casting range, but seeing them nonetheless, which is a small triumph even on good days. With a little help from the weather we could have caught some, I think, for they were rooting for crabs and shrimp as voraciously as Shriners at a free buffet. And I was armed with The Fly—a modified Gotcha tied with arctic fox fur and a few secret sprinkles that fly-design alchemist George Roberts had sent me, and which outfished every pattern in my box by ten to one, at least on bonefish. I'm certain the permit would have fallen all over it, too . . . with just a few breaks in the weather.

But we got few breaks in the weather, Carlos and I, and we spent much of our time huddled in the boat in our oilskins, hanging from the anchor in deep water or from the pole thrust into the mud in the shallows, waiting for the squall of the moment to pass us by, trying to make ourselves too small and insignificant to attract the lightning that flashed everywhere around us, bailing with a plastic bucket and talking of our past lives as commercial fishermen, of our grown sons and our worries for their futures, of how we prefer to do things for ourselves—build our own lobster traps, our own boats, our own houses—because we can't bear to spend good money for indifferent work. Neither of us likes being disappointed by others.

One day, as we sat between squalls eating lunch and watching the broad undulating backs of leopard rays gliding by in our lee, two tarpon better than a hundred pounds cruised downwind toward the boat, reversing course only a few feet away with a swirl and a splash before I could even think of reaching for a rod. Carlos merely shook his head sadly. "You got to be ready," he said. "Always got to be ready. This like hunting, not fishing."

On another day, grounded in six inches of water and two feet of mud while waiting out yet another screaming gale, dozens of feeding bones swam near the boat, their fins and tails and sleek dark backs knifing through the roiled water like surfaced submarines on parade. I tried casting to them, but in the wild gusts all I could do was frighten them away a bit farther from the boat. "Maybe you work a bit more on your casting," Carlos had said, sadly shaking his head. "Follow through bit more maybe; doan stop the rod so high like trouts fisherman." I nodded and smiled and promised to do better, for I did not want to disappoint Carlos.

That night at supper, I was guiltily pleased that two Ambergris Cay habitués—Don, a corporate headhunter on his fourth trip here, a cross between John Kenneth Galbraith and Mister Rogers, and Rich, a Manhattan architect on his eighth trip here, a cross between Frank Zappa and Groucho Marx—had fared little better than I did. They too had given up on the visibility-impaired tarpon flats and had gone after bones, spooking many and catching few in the frustrating winds and leaden skies. We took pleasure, the three of us, in our mutual incompetence. And in the lobster salad and conch fritters doused with Marie Sharp's Habañero Pepper Sauce, whose pre-Columbian fires we extinguished with a sufficiency of Belikin Mayan Temple Beer.

Despite its new tourist-economy veneer, Ambergris Cay today seems not all that far from the Mayan world. In its heyday this was an important trading outpost for the Mayans. The cay—actually not a true cay but part of the Yucatán Peninsula severed from the Mexican mainland by a canal dug by the Mayans around A.D. 600—sits just inside the barrier reef that protects this low sandy spit of land and the commerce that furrows the broad bay beyond. In centuries past, large Mayan trading canoes plied these waters, carrying salt and fish, cacao and slaves. Today, on the high-priced ocean side with its miles of sugar-sand beaches, an endless parade of boat traffic fills the waters: everything from snarling overpowered outboards and patchwork-propelled sloops sprung from the pages of Peter Matthiessen's *Far Tortuga* to extraterrestrial fiberglass catamarans from a French charter company, their broad gleaming decks draped with overfed and incompletely clad pink Parisians on holiday.

Ambergris Cay seems more than anything like Venice, only not sinking into the sea and very much in the Third World and just shy of aggressively hot—though it's worth noting that in July it's usually a good ten degrees cooler than New York City. On the leeward side of the cay, miles of creeks and canals intertwine through endless mangroves split here and there by the back porches and private docks of the residents. Everyone goes everywhere by boat, and all day long the children swim like otters. Ambergris Cay enjoys as nearly amphibious a culture as you will find this side of Atlantis. It makes you wish for gills and webbed feet.

The cay's mini metropolis of San Pedro—named, as you would expect from an oceanic outpost that has long thrived on its cornucopia of fish, for the patron saint of fishermen—is a tight cluster of pastel dwellings, intriguing odorous shops, and shiny new hotels that sprout like mushrooms after a rain.

The cay's people show the mingled features and habits of the various cultures that have at one time or another occupied this thin rim of sand and trees: the Mayans, of course, and the Spanish who came here in the sixteenth century; the French, Dutch, and English pirates who hid out here in the eighteenth century, and the British colonists who arrived in the early nineteenth and retained ownership until 1981, when the Crown colony of British Honduras became the independent nation of Belize.

English, not surprisingly, is the lingua franca of Belize, but the Belizean people don't really speak English; they sing it, in a cheery lilting burble that makes our own uncouth utterances sound like the croaks of asthmatic ravens. Every morning I asked shy willowy Edith, who looks like Audrey Hepburn seasoned with a dash of Nancy Kwan and a spritz of Olive Oyl, about the breakfast special that El Pescador's menu urged us to ask about but which never quite seemed to materialize, at least not until a large and garrulous party of intensely prosperous anglers arrived to supplement the indolent and decidedly shabby trio of Don and Rich and me. And every morning she answered, or more accurately sang in her soft rhythmic lilt, "*No.* Dere is *no* speshul to-*day*. Maybe you have some bay-*cone?* And Spawnish ahm-*lette?* An English muh-*fin?* Some man-*go?* Pa-pie-*ya?* Pie-na-*pul?* Goooo-*ooood?* Ooohhh-kay."

The whole place sings: The mangroves sing with hooded orioles, warblers, vireos, catbirds, hummingbirds; the flats crackle with the castanet carapaces of crabs and shrimp and the sizzle of speeding bonefish. After a while you just want to loll on the beach under a coconut palm, soaking in the music, mooning at the stars, and scheming ways to go Gauguin.

Then came a day when sun in the east floodlit the soggy black behinds of clouds fleeing toward the west—the weary remnants of the storm that after a week of hanging just off the coast had finally come ashore in the night howling like a Shop-Vac swallowing a cat, fire-hosing the hotel with hard-edged raw ocean, and sending coconuts and lawn chairs flying around like soccer balls.

And a perfect day followed, though of course it was my last day, which is why I spent more of it with a camera than with a fly rod, a not-so-minor drawback of fishing for a living instead of fishing for fun. And not one easily avoided.

"You not going to fish? Just going to take peectures? Aii-yi-yi. Such a good day," Carlos said, shaking his head wearily. "Just enough wind. We see a lot of fish when there is no wind, but the fish they doan want to take. Too much wind and you doan see no fish. Today just right. You sure you doan want to fish?"

"I can't until I get some useful photographs. This is my last chance. I wanna follow Rich and Don around a while, see if they get something, and maybe you can do some fishing, too."

"No problem. I fish all you want. I do that for some guys from Ee-Es-Pee-Ens down here last year. They doan do nothing but take pic-tures, too."

We started the day as always drifting off Cangrejo, where Don jumped a good tarpon but lost it to a freak butt wrap, then Rich hung into another good one and lost it in the way you would expect to lose an angry fish the size of a bear with a mouth as hard as horn that de-cides to unsportingly rush the boat instead of the horizon as it ought.

"Those guys there," Carlos said, nodding over at Rich snoozing in the sun and Don intent in the bow and Nesto poling slowly in the stern, "they having a good day. Already they hook two fish and this before lunch. Some days nobody hook nothing, nobody see nothing. You sure you doan want to fish?"

"Pictures, Carlos. I got to get pictures. Got to get paid. Got to make a living." And Carlos shook his head sadly.

An hour later, with the likelihood of jumping a tarpon off Cangrejo diminishing with every degree the sun ratcheted into the sky, we headed back down to Savannah Cay and found the water ice clear and tarpon ghosting here and there. We worked slowly along with the wind and sun at our backs, finally setting up an ambush where thin fingers led from the deep blue channel onto the pale green flats.

A school with a good fifty fish swept in from the sea, and Carlos leapt to the bow, expertly fired out a big Cockroach with my twelve-weight, and hooked a forty-pounder, wrestling it boatside just as the hook pulled free. Then he quickly hooked another, perhaps a little bigger, and lost it just as Rich had earlier, the tarpon running unfairly toward the boat instead of honestly and predictably away from it. Then Rich, a hundred yards away, replayed almost the same scene, though he got two good jumps before the tarpon rushed the boat and threw the hook. Then another tarpon, at least twice the size of the others, charged the boat so fast that by the time we saw him he was passing ten feet in front of the bow and accelerating past thirty knots. Then Carlos was into another fish, and from across the water came the sound of Rich's reel screeching like an F-16.

It went on like that into the early afternoon then abruptly shut down—just at the time I figured I had enough photographs to skate by and could trade camera for fly rod, of course.

Carlos shook his head sadly. "You should have fished when the fish were here."

"Photos, Carlos. I had to get photos. Make my living. Pay my bills."

And Carlos shook his head sadly. "Should fish when the fish are here," he said.

We hunted unsuccessfully around Mosquito Cay then ran back toward Cangrejo and saw a huge school of jack crevalle, maybe four hundred fish in the twenty-pound range tearing up the water, but we lost them in a squall that leapt from nowhere, shuttering off the sun and glazing over the sea with a sere gray veil.

Then we ducked back onto the bonefish flats and took turns casting to them, each of us taking six or seven including a couple pushing five pounds—good bones for Belize. The wind continued to rise, though, which made it almost impossible for Carlos to maneuver the heavy twenty-three-foot skiff with the pole and made casting into the wind like casting against a brick wall; casting downwind launched an uncontrolled line length at the mere flick of the wrist. I'm sorry to say that I took some pleasure when Carlos had as much trouble as I did hitting the erratic speeding dinner plate that is a cruising bonefish's strike zone, and when he lost just as many fish as I did to the tiny jutting mangroves that sawed through leaders with a soft, inevitable *snat*.

Between gusts an enormous permit hove into view some seventy feet crosswind, and I plotted angles and sniffed the breeze and wound out a beautiful tight-looped sizzler that boinked that permit right in the head with George's magic Gotcha.

"Ai-yi-yi. You got to *lead* the fish, not cast right at them," Carlos said, shaking his head.

The next day, heading down the dock for the airport water taxi, I shook hands with Carlos and pressed into his palm what I hoped was the right number of compensatory Dead Presidents, and I got in the boat and sped away, not looking back for fear that once more I had disappointed Carlos.

8

And When I Died

Will you calm down? You're not going to let a little near-death experience ruin your mood, are you?

—WOODY ALLEN, *Antz*

s I have written before but promise not to again, when I was just entering my teens I briefly abandoned fly fishing for trout with my father and brother in favor of bait fishing for catfish with a gang of river rats who were uncharitably characterized by the parental wing of our fly-fishing sect as lowlifes and no-'counts. Hormonally driven toward adolescent acts of defiance, I wanted to do battle with great fierce leviathans that could snarf my dignified father's sissy little mountain trout as insouciantly as a baleen whale filters krill. And because I'm a southerner, a self-destructive subspecies of North American male whose most common last words are "Hey, y'all watch this," I wanted to flirt with danger in a conspicuously flamboyant fashion.

And I also had something to prove, if not to others then certainly to me: A few summers before I had drowned, or very nearly. I got to that TV talk-show point where everything glowed white, and Bach fugues swelled to an E. Powerful Biggsian crescendo that overwhelmed even the Tennessee River thundering a hundred feet down through the hydroelectric turbines of Fort Loudoun Dam, an implacable wall of concrete towering directly over my head. But just as I seemed to rise up into the mist and look down on what had been me sinking limply into the foam, one of those no-'count river rats my father privately and my mother openly scorned hauled me aboard his johnboat, and I awoke miles downriver at Fate Evans's boat dock in comforting paramedical arms. As I looked around at worried gaunt faces peppered with stubble and Beechnut and Day's Work, I heard someone say, "Hail, 'at there's Doc Babb's boy. I wudden wanna be him when *he* gits home." And then I almost wished I had gotten on board that train a-comin' rather than having to trudge home and explain to my red-faced mother how I came to lose my glasses and shoes and fishing rod and why a reporter from the *Lenoir City News* was knocking on her door asking for a statement from the nearly bereaved.

Partly I wanted to get back on this horse what flung me, and by so doing perhaps vanquish demons and be able again to swim and submerge my face without that blind strangling panic that even today sometimes rushes in, triggered by such inconsequential aquatic events as the water pump kicking in and the shower blasting my face with the memory of hydroelectric turbines that spew tons of water at the robotic whim of an Alcoa aluminum smelter's thermostat. And partly I wanted to get back up under that dam because, of course, that's where the big ones live.

I couldn't hazard a guess how many anglers die each year in daring expeditions to the places where the big ones live. It's rare for the western

stonefly hatch to pass without a casualty—an overconfident wader
surging one rock too far; an incautious wader floundering mothlike
toward the flame of a splashing rise; an inexperienced wader suddenly
sensing trouble and turning to go back, standing momentarily square
to the flow then with hydraulic inevitability sweeping downstream, his
waders filling and his thoughts turning to home and family and the
wader belt he belatedly realizes wasn't a mere fashion affectation.

And then there are the rickety old floatplanes some of us pile
hopefully into, which drone across Arctic barrens with seats as hard
and cold as tombstones. We sit there watching the fuselage flex
against its temporarily permanent scaffolding of duct tape and randomly riveted sheet tin, trying not to remember that DeHavilland
made these planes about the same time many of our parents made
us, trying not to think that lodges mostly operate on thin margins
and economize where prudent and sometimes where not, focusing
our minds instead on wild leaping charr and salmon that seldom see
an angler and hoping we will live long enough for them to see us and
we them. And the horseback rides that skirt yawning canyons, where
a stick masquerading as a rattlesnake or a cliff-edge bush promising
exotic new edibility may be the last thing either the horse or you will
ever see. And the airboats blasting through twisting cypress-swamp
channels that intertwine unannounced and sometimes spit out other
blasting airboats piloted, like ours, by an anxious angler looking neither right nor left but only straight ahead toward bass tearing into a
school of threadfin a half mile distant. And those long, long offshore
runs in boats we know are too small on days we know we should not
go but do anyway because the giant bluefin are running, and we
catch one first thing and—driven by the smell of overheated reel
drags—hunt through the day for another, refusing to see the hard
gray line building in from the southeast because, after all, we're way
out there where the big ones live.

And so I found myself back inside one of those yawning turbine holes, brought there this time not by the sweeping backcurrent that had plucked me from the bank behind the DANGER NO TRESPASSING fence I had squeezed under but by J. D.'s stout johnboat. I tried to think only of catfish and not of my twelve-year-old head bobbing up and down not six feet from where we sat. I tried not to think that between the day that dam first closed its gates in 1943 and the day I made my second trip up inside it, two dozen anglers flush with lunatic daring had died doing exactly what we were doing—about one and a quarter deaths there for each year it had been possible to die there, and all for catfish. Those enormous, ugly, magnificent catfish.

Since then I have tried with varying degrees of success to explain to others over campfires and dinner tables the relationship between anglers and danger in general, and hydroelectric dams and southern males in particular, but have never done so to my satisfaction, for after all I am explaining these things less to them than to me. Permit me a final attempt.

A hydroelectric dam on the TVA model gulps water from its upstream side and jets it downhill through tubular penstocks to giant turbines, spinning blades that in turn spin electric generators. The water exits through a flume that arcs down to the bottom and pierces a series of rectangular recesses cut into the dam's face. To reduce erosion, the exhaust cants very slightly upward and exits over a concrete apron that ends in a slight lip, over which the discharged water boils up like a fountain. In the lee of this apron shelter inconceivable numbers of fish, drawing anglers up into those turbine holes as magnetically as a big brown rising to adult stones draws a Madison River fly fisher one step past fail-safe.

Getting inside the turbine holes is a high-wire act without a net. Because the turbines are demand-driven, the first warning that they've kicked on is a hard-edged wall of water that fills the holes and turns anything inside into matchsticks and pink jelly. After the initial explosion, the outrushing water bores a hole in the river and boils up about eight feet downstream, leaving the inside of the hole as calm as a millpond. This is why you enter only generating turbines. You thread between two boils with the motor wide open and the moment precisely timed, lest the complex currents flip you like a flapjack. Once past the boils you angle into a hole and back down sharply; then you slam into the maintenance-gate channels at the front edges of the hole a pair of stout oak poles iron-strapped to your gunnel's top edges. This holds you securely athwart the hole and lets you fish the boils as safe as houses—unless the turbine cuts off. Then you need to get downriver fast, because an imbalance in turbine flows sets up a swift-sweeping back eddy that can make exiting a hole as uncertain as high-stepping a high wire in a hurricane. Not to mention, an automatic turbine that suddenly kicks off can just as suddenly kick back on.

I say all the above entirely for my catharsis and your amusement and not for your instruction, though anyone attempting to poke his boat inside a hydroelectric dam based entirely on the scanty information presented here is probably well out of the gene pool anyway.

Stuffed into the cool dark shade of Number One turbine, the closest to the bank and thus the best fishing but also the most dangerous to enter and exit, we rigged whole shad on our big hooks and let the deep-sea sinkers carry them out into the boils. As we waited for the soft dull thud of a flathead mouthing the bait I felt J. D.'s eyes on me. He had been here the day the back eddy pulled me off the bank, and along with two other johnboats filled with no-'count low-life river rats had come up behind the boils looking for me. They had swept back and forth through the wild swirling currents, trying to see where I'd gone, and finally old Willard Parks saw something, gunned his johnboat through the boils, reached way down into the water with a tuna gaff and hooked me aboard. J. D. had seen my face then, pale and sagging and leaking water, and he saw my face now, pale and pinched and haunted by water. He listened to the jokes I too stridently told, understanding, as men who have been boys do, that I wanted more than anything else in the world for him not to know I was scared out of my mind, wanted him not to know that for the past two years I had been dragged from sleep again and again by the weight of water and concrete towering over my head, by the sound of turbine blades whirring and heavy water boiling, the turbine blades that whirred only a dozen feet behind and above where we sat in his johnboat and the water that boiled and roared like Icelandic magma a bare rod length away.

We caught fish, as I remember—nothing spectacular, nothing like the hundred-pounders that come out from under Number One turbine every now and then, but good enough to have made it worth the trip, if I add to the balance with the stringers of potbellied catfish the slow encysting of memory in layers of psychic callus. We went up under the dam a dozen or so times over that summer and the next, and the third summer I began to sleep through the night without waking wheezing and wet. Finally I drifted away from the big river and back into the mountains for a time, and by the fourth year I had drifted even farther away to the shores of a cold broad ocean where I wore navy blue and lived, but barely, through a boot-camp torture called Abandon Ship Drill.

Every time I go back home I stop by that dam and look down into the waters where I died and was reborn—hypnotized by water and terrified by water, but always compelled to be on the water, to be looking at water, hearing water, thinking of water. I climb down the bank and on the safe side of the safety fence look up into the turbine holes, no longer seeing any fishermen I specifically recognize nearly forty years hence but still seeing plenty I generally recognize: no-'count low-life river rats who dare to go up inside, up under there where the big ones live and where others sometimes die. And I think: Someday I'll try that again, going up under that dam, perhaps with a fourteen-weight and a lead-core shooting head and a shark-worthy Clouser with dumbbell eyes and a smear of shad guts for savor. And maybe, up there where the big ones live, I might tangle with the ultimate leviathan and finally vanquish those dreams. Then I think of the weight of all that water poised above my head and the turbine blades whirring and the river roaring like a Wagnerian opera gone insane, and the grasping-at-life timidity that rules middle age kicks in as automatically as a hydroelectric turbine, and I turn back toward the mountains, to the musical knee-deep streams where I have always fished and always felt safe and happy, and have never yet died.

Third
Movement

Autumn

O suns and skies and clouds of June,
And flowers of June together,
Ye cannot rival for one hour
October's bright blue weather.

—HELEN HUNT JACKSON, *Verses*

9

The Coriolis Effect

Single-mindedness is all very well in cows or ba-
boons; in an animal claiming to belong to the same
species as Shakespeare it is simply disgraceful.

—ALDOUS HUXLEY, *Do What You Will*

" About two minutes," Bill hollered back from the cockpit. I dropped my book and my end of polite conversation, snatched a look at the scrolling electronic map with its cartoon airplane nosing up to a thin lateral bisection and out the window toward Ecuador sliding past green and peaky thirty-five thousand feet below, and headed aft for the head to indulge an obsession.

"Okay," Bill's voice crackled over the intercom. ". . . two, three, four, *now.*" I flushed. And saw pet theories sluiced down the chute.

But I wasn't about to be foiled by a bunch of French aerospace engineers unwilling simply to let gravity do its job, so I spun around and filled the sink and then pressed DRAIN, and the little whirlpool hesitated for a second and then curled back around against the clock, just as Gustave-Gaspard de Coriolis said it would way back in 1835.

"How'd it go?" folks asked as I returned to my seat.

"Not well," I said. "The cultural imperialists who designed this airplane angled the toilet drain so it's always in the Northern Hemisphere no matter where the plane is. They forgot about the sink, though; it has no engineered biases and proves the theory perfectly: The vortex spirals clockwise north of the line and counterclockwise south of the line. But after all that playing with the toilet I was too late to try it *on* the line. On the way home, though, I'll fill that sink to the scuppers well before we get to the equator and I'll push the drain button just as we hit the line. By my calculations it'll jet straight down."

Harry said, "You need to get a life."

And I said, "Harrumph. This from the man who's been trout fishing in Chile three times and never noticed whether the rise rings swirled clockwise or counterclockwise."

Harry just shook his head. I'd been interrogating him about Chilean rise rings since we'd left Alabama that morning and in a flurry of inquisitional faxes even before. I was sure he was holding out on me about which way the rings spiral, though for what reason I could not yet fathom. But ahead of us was a week on the Futaleufu River in the Patagonian Andes, and by all accounts there'd be trout rising as far as the eye could see. And all of those rise rings, according to this theory I'd caught but could not seem to release, would swirl counterclockwise. I'd get to the bottom of this or annoy everyone around me trying.

"When the trout in my pond snarf kibbles," I told everyone still pretending to listen, "the swirl goes clockwise. In the Northern Hemisphere air flows out from a center of high pressure in a clockwise circulation, and air flowing into a center of low pressure—a hurricane, for instance—veers counterclockwise. South of the equator it reverses. If the Coriolis effect governs hurricanes and plumbing drains, why not trout? And dogs? When my dog hits the sack, she circles her bed with the clock. So does my friend Byron's dog down in Tennessee. Only once did I see Madison circle counterclockwise, and that after his housemate, Gibbon, had beat hell out of him for trying to sneak into her bed. Wow, has the *lodge* got a *dog*? Did you ever notice which way it circles when it goes to *bed*?"

I was getting excited now, but my fellow travelers were looking for polite ways of changing the subject. Obsessions, I have to keep reminding myself, are only interesting to those who have them.

Like many members of my annoying generation, I catch obsessions the way normal people catch colds, and like colds most last a week if indulged or seven days if ignored. For many people fly fishing is an obsession, but having acquired the habit before the onset of sentience, fly fishing is for me more an involuntary act of everyday living, like sleeping or eating or watching reruns of *The Simpsons*. Subsets within fly fishing certainly qualify as obsessions, and over the years I have fallen prey to an endless parade of what my dad used to call "another one of Jimmy's crazes"—my flirtation with Deep Entomology; my elbows-and-arseholes exact-imitation-dry-fly-only era; my lead-mine-trout-dredging days; my Tiparillo-puffing green-Dickie-wearing Crusty Mainer streamer-flinger period; my three big gaudy wet flies dangled downstream off a long cane rod retrograde; my long-range artillery duels with big-bore Spey rods and 500-grain salt-water shooting heads; my . . . well, you get the picture: Every trend that comes along, I'll be there, like Tom Joad or Cher. Only two obsessions have stuck fast over the years: a passionate belief in small anonymous trout streams as High Church, and the sure knowledge that I'd trade every day of fishing throughout the year for the brief golden weeks of autumn.

Far more than the belief that if trout rises swirl clockwise north of the equator then they must swirl counterclockwise south of it, it was this obsession with the fall of the year that drew me toward Chile in April—this rare chance to live a year with not one crisp autumn but two. Well, that and Bob calling and asking if I wanted to go fishing in Chile, and me saying I'd like to but couldn't afford it and anyway just for curiosity's sake what would it cost, and him saying Not much 'cause we'll fly down in his airplane and the lodge owner, Jim Repine, had invited me to be his personal guest, and me saying Whoa, I'm there dude. Or words to that effect; people who fly their own jets, I've found, rarely enjoy being called dude.

And so we rendezvoused in Montgomery, Alabama—Bob and his wife, Helen, and Bill and Dick the pilots (Bob was piloting, too, airplanes being his obsession), and Dick's wife, Liz, and our friend Harry in from Houston, and me and my belief that if drains reverse their spirals when crossing the equator then trout must, too—and we headed way south, flying over Cuba toward an overnight in Guayaquil, Ecuador, then on to Puerto Montt, Chile, paralleling the soaring Andes so jaggedly Lovecraftian that if the Rocky Mountains ever saw them they'd shrivel into sad sniveling stubs, and me trying all the way not to let my obsession du jour drive everyone around me as crazy as it was driving me.

And I was also trying to stifle those motormouth social indiscretions that become for me a kind of Tourette's syndrome whenever I inadvertently find myself around what Huck Finn called "the quality": What *about* this global warming? I want to demand, waving my arms and rolling my eyes and foaming at the mouth like someone who doesn't himself drive a pollution-pooting old pickup truck and is hitching a free ride on a private jet. And have you *seen* the latest figures on the increasing concentration of *wealth* in the hands of the *few* and the dissolution of the middle *class*? I want to know from less hypocritical ground. And don't even get me *start*ed on the minimum *wage*, which adjusted for in*fla*tion is *half* what it was in 19 70. And how come a *poor* man goes to prison for *five years* for stealing milk for his *kids* while billionaire CEOs of outlaw multi*na*tionals get caught fixing *pri*ces and greasing poli*ti*cians and are just told *Tsk*, don't get caught doing *that* again or it'll be three months of intensive *ten*nis camp with nothing but screw-cap *wine* to wash down the foie *gras* and what will the *share*holders *think. And . . . And . . .* You get the picture.

The thing is, writers and painters and other optional artistic garnishes have to throttle our wild-eyed egalitarian urges when we're around the kinds of people who actually have the money to buy the stuff we have to sell. Sharing art with the world is a beautiful thing, but not if it leaves you flipping burgers to buy your typewriter ribbons and paintbrushes. When class-warfare push comes to accommodationist shrug, most of us underfunded artistic types swallow our pride and buck and wing a double-haul shuffle whenever Ole Massah wants entertaining. At least those of us not blessed with trust funds or inconveniently inflexible principles do, especially when a free trip to Chile beckons.

But I obsess. And not even about autumn, which is what I started to obsess about before being overtaken by . . . Well, another one of Jimmy's crazes. And so back to autumn, which, as is the case with most things worth being crazed about, starts with spring.

Where I live in Maine, spring is like peasant life in the bad old days of feudalism: nasty, brutish, and short. You know spring is coming, you're convinced it's here, and then it snows a foot and the robins beat their brains out drilling for worms in freeze-dried soil and then come stare at you through the windows with big weepy eyes like it's all your fault. A sunny day comes lilting in on sweet burbling birdsong and that whispered warmth that swells all the world with pantheistic lust, and before midmorning a cold gale hisses in off the frigid ocean and shrivels tumescent apple buds to pink peppercorns and your 'nads to Birdseye peas. A Maine spring is like a Christmas present from a wealthy great-aunt you've never met and hear from only on holidays: endlessly anticipated, beautifully wrapped, and in the end a crushing disappointment—the climatological equivalent of expecting a Lionel train or at least a John Gnagy Learn-to-Draw Set and finding only tube socks and whitey-tighty underwear a size too small.

Give me autumn, I say, with the blackflies and tourists all gone with the wind, and the leaves just tingeing crimson and gold, and the trout trading their springtime paranoia for bacchanalian autumnal feasting, bulking up like everyone and everything in New England for the long gestational winter. Give me autumn. Give me endless autumns, or at least the chance, now and then, to score a cut-rate invitation to a bihemispherical double dip.

It was autumn for certain when we landed in Puerto Montt, clean and clear and crisp and deliciously cool after the mildewed tropical squalor of Ecuador. Bob and Helen and Harry and I piled into an aged Sky-King-to-Flying-Crown-Ranch twin Cessna for the mountain-bumping flight into the village of Futaleufu, while Bill and Dick and Liz put the Falcon to bed and headed for Puerto Montt and a week of unsupervised tourism.

We climbed steadily over Norwegianesque fjords toward those great tangled mountains, so raw and new and flagrantly geologic—these glacier-glazed Krazy-Kones of ancient granite and gneiss, these prolapsed caldera sprouting erectile cones from their wanton cores. Flying ever onward and upward toward ever more of the same, I began to imagine we were Conway and Barnard and Mallinson and Miss Brinklow from James Hilton's *Lost Horizon*, flown by mysterious means toward some unknown Shangri-La past mountains of "fearsome spectacle," for there was "something raw and monstrous about those uncompromising ice-cliffs, and a certain sublime impertinence in approaching them thus."

There was no place en route for an emergency landing should those mountains take exception to our impertinence, not even a convenient place to crash, at least not where searchers could ever come sift through our dust for souvenirs. And then just as I began obsessing about my poor widowed wife weeping alone in the dark for three mournful months before going timorously off into the world to marry a rich mesomorph who's inexhaustible in bed and doesn't fart under the covers then giggle about it, we finally leveled off, skirting a mountain so close I could count individual fibers of lichen etched into scoured ledge. Harry said, "This is the coolest part; watch this," and the plane pivoted with one wingtip anchored to a great loom of granite and dropped like a stone—peeling off and plummeting like an F-86 diving on MiGs over the Yalu River, then at the last minute leveling off and almost instantly crunching onto a short gravel runway that split the center of a sweet virgin valley as perfectly hidden in its nest of towering mountains as a clutch of owlets in a hemlock.

We piled into a Pathfinder, stuffing its tagalong trailer with enough luggage to support a three-ring circus, and set off through a manicured and freshly swept alpine village where horses and wagons outnumbered automobiles and fading rosebushes peeked over yard fences like the phytogenic aftermath of a Pasadena parade. We had flown from the twenty-first century into the early twentieth, and before we were a mile from town we slid back into the seventeenth, for the road soon shrank into what looked like an oxcart path, and then on cue around the next bend there appeared an oxcart straight out of a Brueghel, its more or less round wheels mere biscuits hacked raw from tremendous trees, its cargo a flock of sheep tied by the ankles and woven into the rough wooden cart like a braid of garlic, its drovers brandishing whips and wearing costumes from a yellowed issue of *National Geographic*, the oxen as massively phlegmatic as a yoke of circus elephants.

And after that the road *really* got bad as we climbed out of the Valley of the Kings, as Harry said it was called, and descended through dense forest deep into the Valley of the Stairs. "Jim and his crew built it with shovels," Harry said about the road. "And a little dynamite. This is a new road. The old one followed the river up over the mountain and it was really bad. Scary in places. Dropped straight down."

And then we came to the river that had brought us all this way, flowing as clear as crystal and as clean as the inside of a microchip factory; not overpowering like the mountains but accessible, comprehensible, and fishably friendly. The driver blew the horn and the far bank filled with tan women in white aprons, shading their eyes and hallooing and waving their arms and crying " 'Arry, 'Arry," and 'Arry waved back and pointed to a hand-lettered sign on the far bank that said WELCOME HOME HARRY as he shouted something exuberantly Spanish.

A driftboat shoved off from the far shore to fetch us to the lodge. As we ferried across the current and backed into a slow-swirling eddy as deep and transparent as a Florida sinkhole, a nice rainbow rose theatrically, though sensory overload kept me from noting which way the ring revolved.

We walked up a pebble-paved path patrolled by poultry and edged by marigolds, at the end of which sat a small white farmhouse, with others of its ilk dotted across a little valley tightly cosseted by soaring mountains, their forested sides too steep to scale, their skinned granite tonsures freshly flecked with snow. Regimental rows of Lombardy poplars just verging into autumn gold divided fields as Gallically green as a Norman estate. Apple trees weeping-willowed beneath the weight of fruit, while a lone pig with its mouth full waited for gravity to deliver another. A ramshackle barn groaned with new loose hay and horses wanting to know who had come and what it meant for them. Sheep baaaaaaahed and baaaaaaahed, inquiring, perhaps, after three of their late relatives spread-eagled on medieval-looking iron swords thrust into the ground before a roaring fire, where an active mustachioed man in a blinding white shirt mopped their crisping flesh with the secret emoluments of *asado,* the classic Chilean barbecue.

Condors spiraled high overhead—counterclockwise, I noted quickly in my spiral-ring—and the towering mountains fired orange in the setting sun. As the shadows lengthened, small knots of people converged on the lodge from all directions—some walking, wearing shawls and home-knitted serapes and Cisco Kid hats decorated with fringes of colored balls like the windshields of a Manila jitney; some riding horses as tricked out with sheepskin-upholstered saddles and intricately carved wooden stirrups as anything that ever swept out of Asia and across the steppes with asset acquisition and gene dispersal in mind. In the barn, lanterns twinkled over long trestle tables that formed an inverted U, their tops draped in white and dotted with dishes. Cattle lowed in the distance to the clapped syncopation of copper bells, and the fire showered sparks on crucified lambs that smelled like heaven on a platter: *Jurassic Park* meets *How Green Was My Valley. The Land That Time Forgot* meets *The Egg and I. Green Acres* meets *The Last Supper.*

"Whaddya think?" Harry said.

All I could do was shake my head and drop my jaw and say, like Beavis eyeing his first nekkid woman, "Whoa. This is the coolest thing I've ever seen."

We had come to the Valley of the Stairs out of sequence, arriving on the night most guests leave and leaving a week later on the day before most guests arrive. Fifty-three hundred miles due north in Mont-

gomery, Bob and Helen had calendarically conflicting social obliga-
tions with some kind of springtime ritual involving boutonnieres and
yards of pink chiffon.

And because we were out of sequence, Harry said, we had arrived
just in time for the fiesta.

At the end of his guests' week on the Futaleufu and Espolon
Rivers, lodgemeisters Jim and Sonia Repine throw a party and invite
the entire valley. Everyone comes, all seventy-five inhabitants. And
this was an especially festive fiesta, because the people of the Valley
of the Stairs had not just four departing guests to fete but four arriving ones as well.

After we had stowed our gear, washed our faces, shaken innumerable hands, and sampled in varying degrees something called a Pisco
Sour—a surprisingly intoxicating concoction of lime juice and sugar
and brandy made from the intensely grapey *pisco* that grows in the
high Chilean desert—we headed off to the barn to join the festivities.
We sat at the head table with Jim and Sonia and the confusingly
named Bill and Bob, the guides brought down from New Hampshire
and Montréal; the valley's other large landowner and his beaming
wife, whose names were too authentically Spanish to penetrate my
thick East Tennessee skull; and the other four American guests who
were leaving tomorrow, one of whom, C. D. Clarke, had just ridden
into town for his phone messages and in one of those coincidences
that are too weird for anything but real life had come back with a
commission from The Lyons Press for the cover of this book.

Smiling women brought great groaning platters of salads and
breads and the *asado* lambs, and we ate like Ottoman potentates
and drank wine like cardinals, the whole barn a din of laughter and
shouting and lip-smacking gusto.

Then the plates disappeared along with the side wings of the
U-shaped table, someone brought out a boombox, fired up some un-

mistakably Spanish music, and, with hands clapping, heels clacking, handkerchiefs slapping, and serapes swirling, the crowd began to dance—young girls dancing with old men, old ladies dancing with small boys, Chilean subsistence farmers in homemade clothing dancing the night away with visiting Americanos who fly their own jets.

After a few days at Jim's lodge, it's easy to see why Harry is so obsessed with this place, why he comes down here year after year, why he sits in his office in Houston and looks longingly south. It's not just the fishing. Though there are exceptions, especially farther south in Tierra del Fuego, which may have the best freshwater fishing on the planet, most of Patagonia's trout fishing can find its equal in lots of places, from Tennessee to Montana, Alberta to New Zealand. But what is hard to match elsewhere, whether on the Chilean or Argentinean side of the border, is Patagonia's feeling of being truly in another world, raw and new yet at the same time old, a world so far unstained and uncrumpled by the grubbing hand of humankind but with civilizing classical touches brought from Europe centuries ago. That this comparative environmental pristinity and time-capsule preservation derive less from a population who chooses to live in harmony with nature and ancient customs than from a population who simply hasn't gotten around to gouging out nature's wealth and building a Wal-Mart on civilization's bones doesn't matter. What does matter is that for whatever reason it hasn't happened here. Yet. Perhaps parts of Patagonia really are the last best place, at least for a while, and as such they become less trendy fly-fishing destinations than respectful pilgrimages to the way things were and still ought to be.

Over the week we all fished steadily and caught plenty of fish—nice rainbows throughout the day on nymphs or dries with nymph trailers, good browns in the evenings on large dry flies skittered around. Occasionally we'd glimpse one of the monster browns that hug the bottom and chase foot-long rainbows wild-eyed into the air. Nobody hooked one that I remember, though Harry had tied into a couple on previous trips and in fact did so again the week after Bob and Helen and I left, Harry having elected to stay down another week in what has become his virtual second home.

I do remember which way those rise rings spiraled, however, which was every which way—clockwise, counterclockwise, perfectly spherical emanations from a central point with no Coriolian bias at all. I asked Jim if these were by any chance *French* trout, but he didn't know what I meant and to tell the truth I didn't either, for I was fast onto a new obsession, and this one didn't swim but walked and trotted and sometimes jumped. Moreover, for sheer single-mindedness it had me beat hands down. Or more accurately, hooves down.

The last time I rode a horse I knew I was born to the saddle. I was Roy Rogers on Trigger, the Lone Ranger on Silver, Zorro on Tornado, Joey on Fury. I sat ramrod straight astride his broad muscular back and looked high out over the land, narrowing my gaze at a puff of distant dust then relaxing when my eagle eyes discerned friend approaching and not foe. I remember being conscious of the brute power contained within his massive gray body, and proud of my ability to command and channel this power through my sheer force of will. Then a horsefly buzzed by and he twitched his ears and jerked a little in the harness, and I screamed like a girl, lost my balance, and landed on my head in mud and horse crap. At least so I'm told. I blot that part out. I suppose I should mention that it was my aunt Mandy's old nag, kept for working the mountain hillsides too steep for her narrow-nose John Deere, and that when she lifted me astride the horse it was hitched to a single-bottomed plow, and that I wasn't up there more than a minute before I freaked out, as we used to say in the olden days. I should also mention that at the time I was only five years old.

I was just past fifty and looking forward to my midlife-crisis era when I next rode a horse, and that was forty-one degrees south in the fall of the year in the Valley of the Stairs, heading back over the mountain toward the Valley of the Kings and a Futaleufu River elbow called the Lagoon, where the river cuts through a sheer rock wall and then eddies back slowly and deeply in a great sweeping semicircle like the trout habitat in a well-funded municipal aquarium.

This was the old road—the one the Pathfinder used to crawl across bearing wide-eyed guests before Jim and Company gouged out a longer, less scenic, but ultimately less frightening route into town. In places the old road traverses a sheer cliff that towers vertically overhead on one side and on the other falls just as vertically into the grand canyon of the Futaleufu. Way down there at the point of the V runs the river, a foaming aquamarine thread slicing its way through the raw Andean moonscape, a string of pearls set in magnificent music-box isolation.

It was the kind of trail where you'd want to pair the least experienced rider with the most experienced horse, and that's exactly what I had, I was told: the most experienced horse. My horse was so experienced he needed no input from me at all, which was just as well, for I had but slim acquaintance with Brakes and Go and was still in a fog over the whole steering thing despite much patient tutelage from experienced horsepeople Bob and Helen. And my horse had his own obsession to pursue. Snack-Pack Jack, as I came to call him, never passed an isolated clump of anything remotely edible, whether thistle or pampas grass or rose hips the size of hen's eggs, without stopping for a sample, even if he'd just passed a thousand bushes exactly like the one that suddenly called out to him like leftover Chinese takeout at midnight.

Don't let him do that, Bob and Helen kept saying. And I tried. I pulled back on the reins, clucked my tongue, flapped my stirrups, urged giddyap with my knees, and pulled his head away from the hors d'oeuvre of the moment with what I imagined to be a stern commanding hand. And he'd look around at me and rattle his lips and snort and blow, and then he'd go back to doing exactly what he'd been doing, as though I and my stern commands were of less consequence than a fruit fly. Finally he'd look up, smacking his lips and belching with a gourmand's unabashed enjoyment, and then he'd notice that the other horses, picking their way carefully along the eroded rocky path, had gotten ahead of him, and he'd run like hell to catch up, leaving me clinging to the saddle like Ichabod Crane on the run from Brom Bones, looking down deep into the canyon a footstep away and wondering, should I lose my grip, exactly how far I'd get before I exploded into an alpaca overcoat filled with strawberry ice cream.

The fishing in the Lagoon, and a float trip down the Upper Futaleufu from the Argentinean border the following day, was, like Huck Finn's analysis of *Pilgrim's Progress,* interesting but tough. The weather was wet and cold and blowy, no surprise during the seasonal buildup to winter in the latitudes justifiably called the Roaring Forties back in sailing-ship times, but weather or not, we cast Beadhead Buggers throughout the day and tiny parachutes toward evening, and in one midday bonanza we fished microcaddis to a pod of trout rising to a brush hatch. And despite a summerlong drought that had left the river four feet down we caught satisfying numbers of fine wild rainbows ranging up to twenty-one inches—bright silver torpedoes washed with delicately peppered pastel pink, a fine artistic understatement in a vastly overstated landscape, where everything below tree line glowed an intense polarized green flecked with gold, crimson, and fuchsia.

Over time we nearly forgot the fishing, so obsessed had we all become with the magic of the place—the people so warmly hospitable, so openly friendly, so proud of their land, so genuinely glad to have us visit with no trace of that fawning Uriah Heepishness that so often veils brooding resentment in the tourist-beset corners of the Third World; the farm valley's pastoral self-sufficiency, where everything but wine and soap and toilet paper sprang unprocessed from the soil, where the evening's entrée that emerged crisply succulent from the *casa de humo*—the ubiquitous Chilean smokehouse—had only that morning been a pig staring hopefully up into an apple tree; the indefinable otherness of the Southern Cross gleaming overhead amid a field of unknown stars strangely arranged; the around-the-clock symphony of the nearby river, pushing and shoving its way to the distant sea; the complete absence of noise from all the whirring and blatting mechanizations that steal from the North American wild its quiet calming peace. Given all this, it's hard to focus on the fishing even when it's transcendental—and when a summerlong drought has left it merely excellent and the wind is a raw harbinger of winter, the sheer novelty of new surroundings becomes the focus by default.

But then the sun came out and the skies cleared, and Harry and I caught the fishing fever big time and a dose of impulsive exploration as well. So we mounted up and headed off with José, who along with being chief chef of the *casa de humo* is the head *husaso*, or cowboy. We made for a distant spot C. D. had found the week before while sniffing around for new water that might hold good fish in the drought.

If the ride over the mountain into the Lagoon had been an adventure, then this was an epic, at least for me. We started easily enough, riding out from Jim and Sonia's farm—it's too friendly and laid back and self-contained to call it a mere fishing lodge—past the valley's small schoolhouse, past small farmhouses where the twenty-first century was far away and not at all envied, through high lonely fields dotted with cattle and sheep, through ever smaller gates in ever rangier fences and along ever narrower trails through ever higher fields until finally the trail dwindled to a track and entered a forest that soared overhead like Sequoias in a Pacific park.

I had by now become, if not a good horseman, at least not a pathetic one. My mushy heart had hardened against my poor hungwy wittle horsy and his endless search for snacks, and flush with instructions from my equestrian friends I held his head high as a true horseman should, at least until we began to descend.

"Give him his head," Harry had said when the trail pitched down, "and stand up in your stirrups; shift your weight to the rear as he descends and let him pick the way."

Descend is such a flaccid word. The dictionary says one descends by inclining downward, moving from a higher to a lower place: a 747 gliding down onto the runway, a department store escalator whisking shoppers from housewares to lingerie. When I stood up in my stirrups to help my horse descend, my heels were even with his ears and my head with his tail. I looked like Big Top Pee-Wee plays Man of La Mancha being lowered into a well.

We descended in this fashion for some time, from the high thin pastures where sheep peacefully grazed into the dark exotic depths of a Rangaroan rain forest, dripping and wet and mossy and indescribably strange and beautiful, along a trail that squirmed back and forth and around and down, never more than a hoofprint wide, across blowdown logs hidden in thick undergrowth, under overhanging limbs that scraped my nose as I lay down flat and let the horse have his head in hopes I could keep mine.

And then the trail disappeared altogether, and José drew forth the machete tucked into the small of his back and whacked a way through like Jungle Jim, trending ever downward toward the distant roar of the river at an angle I would have found hard to descend without sitting on my ass and sliding.

And during all this I felt no fear, or at least not much, for I figured any animal as concerned with his stomach as Snack-Pack Jack would never risk anything that might mean missing a meal. It was only after the trail flattened out that I realized he hadn't stopped for a snack since we entered the forest. And it was hours later before I understood what that might mean.

Finally we reached the river and found a long, twisting rapids feeding a knee-deep riffle, a beautifully creased seam, a slow-rolling tongue, and a deep eddying pool where the low-brass section held imperious sway. If I say it was worth the ride I'd be overstating the obvious. The fishing was as good as we'd hoped it would be. Good rainbows and browns were stacked up in the riffle and tongue like commuter planes over O'Hare, and in this almost untouched corner of the lightly fished Futaleufu they were as gullible as hatchery trout chasing PowerBait. We nymphed them, and we streamered them, and we dry-flied them, and we caught and released as many as we wanted and perhaps more than we should. Then we stretched out on the bank and basked in the sun, lunching on sweet-corn tamales and freshly broiled chicken that had yesterday pecked among the marigolds.

And then it was time to head back up the trail. On Harry's advice I was leaning as far forward on the ascent as I had leaned back on the descent, grabbing a handful of mane to, as Harry said, help him climb. And I was feeling quite the accomplished horseman as we made our way up the trail, at least for a while.

Then it soon became apparent that although Snack-Pack Jack had been too worried about his own hide to stop for snacks on the way down, he had nevertheless kept his eyes open and had marked his spots carefully, for on the way back up that hill he never paused at random for a nibble but beelined from tasty bite to tasty bite as unerringly as a yellow jacket at a church picnic.

At first I felt I should indulge his culinary obsessions on the ascent as thanks for letting me live through the descent, but I had forgotten his habit of running to catch up, once he realized the other horses were far ahead, and I had not factored into my tolerance for his bad habits how a horse lunging up a forty-five-degree slope might affect his rider, especially if his rider is me. Still, after I gave up trying to look like a horseman who knew what he was doing and simply wrapped my arms around his neck and my legs around his girth, I did pretty well. But then Snack-Pack Jack came to one of those innumerable blowdowns that crisscrossed the trail, over which he had picked his way carefully on the descent and over which his stablemates had picked their way carefully on the ascent. And he jumped.

I didn't fall all the way off, at least not right away. And I'm not even sure just when I noticed I was clutching a tree instead of my horse. I just know that one minute I was clinging to his side, like a Cheyenne ducking down to shoot arrows at John Wayne, and the next I was hugging a tree and picking leaves out of my teeth.

To his credit, Snack-Pack Jack paused to let me scramble back aboard, and we headed on up the trail in this stop-and-go fashion, a culinary pilgrim's stations of the cross. When we finally got to the top and reentered the high thin pastureland, Harry and José were a long way down the track, and that's when I learned that I had been wrong in saying before that Snack-Pack Jack ran to catch up. He had in fact only been trotting, and there is considerable difference between the two. I know, because when he hit the pasture he took off at an authentic giddyap-the-bad-guys-is-a-gettin'-away gallop. And I stayed on, though I don't know how. Moreover, I even came to like it, not a good sign for someone prone to obsessions. By the time we got back to Jim's farm I had already begun to see horses grazing the pasture back home I resent having to mow, and I imagined pack trips far back into the Maine woods to places too far to walk, too dry to canoe,

and too wet to mountain bike. So far this craze remains safely in its
larval stage, but it can't be a good sign that I'm rereading *Lonesome
Dove* while humming the theme to *The Magnificent Seven.*

Back at the farm on our last night, we sat around the porch sipping
at Pisco Sours and the cool autumn air and telling fish stories. We
talked about obsessions—how people we knew had gone off the deep
end on this, that, or the other wild whim and how all this kept life
fresh and interesting. And we talked about how animals seemed
equally beset by these crazes that grab hold without warning and
don't let go—dogs driven mad by tennis balls or groundhogs, cats by
pipe cleaners or women's underwear hanging on someone else's
clothesline, horses by novel snacks or bright blue golf carts, the three
big rainbows in my pond that had become serially obsessed by tadpoles, crayfish, and newts and spent all their days hunting them with
cold-blooded ferocity while ignoring the Purina trout kibbles that
rained down like manna.

The conversation naturally worked its way around to how Jim had
found his way to southern Chile, and like most interesting lifestyle
changes it all came back to obsessions. Jim had grown up in Virginia
and, like so many American males raised on a steady diet of *Field &
Stream* and *Outdoor Life,* had chased a wilder life into Alaska, the last
best place, as long as you don't notice that each year three hundred
other subscribers to *Field & Stream* and *Outdoor Life* decide to act on
the same obsession. So Jim did the whole guiding and writing trip up
in Alaska as it slowly filled with people just like him, and about ten
years ago he came down to Chile on assignment for the *Anchorage
Daily News* to check out the fishing.

He flew back to Alaska in the grips of a burning obsession, held a
yard sale, and headed back to Chile knowing only six words of Spanish. He met Sonia through a mutual friend with a Yenta complex;

they had lunch together, and he was irrevocably smitten. Obsessed, if you will.

He and Sonia together fell in love with the Futaleufu Valley while researching the river for another lodge a hundred miles on the other side of the mountain. They moved to the town, looked at half a dozen places for sale, and settled on this small farm tucked into a remote valley accessible at that time only by horseback, a farm that just happens to have running by its door the best wadable fishing on one of the best rivers in Patagonia.

Then with the stories at low ebb we all leaned back with our feet up and watched the condors soar, drifting off into our own reveries underpinned by endless river music untarnished by the sound of anything remotely mechanical.

We were nearing the equator when the cockpit called back to alert me for another Coriolian assault, but my nose was buried in a magazine designed to help Nord Americanos relocate themselves and their businesses to Chile, a country with a 1 percent income tax and property taxes you can pay from pocket change, with one of the highest standards of living in South America, with a stable government our CIA is unlikely to re-oust any time soon, with such a highly educated and cultured populace, such phenomenal cuisine, such beautiful doe-eyed people, such grand sweeping scenery and endless miles of trout streams where no one has ever wet a line and, in the fifteen hundred miles of well-watered mountain valleys south of Puerto Montt, that in many cases no one has ever even seen; where predators are rare and biting insects unknown, and lovely Chilean reds that challenge the best from Bordeaux or the Alexander Valley can be had for the price of rotgut-in-a-box, and I only looked up when Bill walked back to tell me again that the equator was coming, and said, *Que?* For after all, the Coriolis effect was last week's obsession.

10

Nature's Call

Country people tend to consider that they have a corner on righteousness and to distrust most manifestations of cleverness, while people in the city are leery of righteousness but ascribe to themselves all manner of cleverness.

—EDWARD HOAGLAND, *Heart's Desire*

I ran into him on a fine September morning about a mile below the campground. I'd been poking along the river and its tributaries for the past week, fishing here and there, living out of my backpack, camping when and where the mood struck, making my way slowly down a series of feeder streams then heading back up the main river to my truck in a wide meandering loop. He was the first human I'd seen all week, and he looked worried.

"How's it goin'?" I said. "Catchin' anything?"

"Not much. A few small brookies I found sipping spinners in the eddies. You?"

"One or two now and then on nymphs, a couple on little olive duns last night."

He was about thirty, dressed drably and neatly, his equipment well chosen, well used, and well cared for: a fly fisherman who clearly had been at it a while and knew what he was about. One of us, I figured, in that judgmental way old-guard fly fishers have of winnowing new acquaintances: not too stylish, no bright colors, no flashing danglies, no Minnie Pearlescent price tags hanging off his vest, circumspect about his success or lack of same, volunteering a bit of useful information but not gushing. One of us.

"So, uh, you fish this river much?" he asked, his eyes darting upriver and down.

"Much as I can."

"Uh, is there, like, a *bath*room near here?"

"Huh?" I said, looking around at the endless evergreen forest, so private, so quiet and inviting now that blackfly season was safely past and the fast-flying September mosquitoes had punched out after their morning shift. "You mean, like, a taking-a-*bath* bathroom? Or are you just looking for a place to crap?"

"Well, I, uh, really have to go," he said, with the embarrassed urgency of a three-year-old missing his diapers. "Bad chili or something. I don't think I can make it back to the campground."

"Hmmmmm, well, bears do it, y'know," I said, thumbing toward the dark enveloping forest. "And I've been doing it all week. Matter of fact, I've been doing it all my life."

"Well, I don't want to pollute anything," he said a little indignantly, "and I don't have any toilet paper."

"Be my guest," I said, handing over the flattened stub end of TP I carry in a Ziploc for emergency evacuations. "Or you could play Mister Natural. I generally look in sunny spots for mullein—it's light green, about waist-high, with broad fuzzy leaves as squeezably soft as Charmin—but ferns are just about as good if you use enough, and they're easier to find in these dark woods," I added, sweeping my rod tip through a waist-high stand. "And you won't pollute a thing. Just go back up there in the woods well above the high-water mark and look for a dry earthy spot that won't hold water after a rain. Dig a little cat hole about eight inches deep, squat down, and fire away. When you're done, fill her back in and cover the spot with leaves and pine needles. It's just gardening. The worms'll turn bad chili into good soil before you know it.

"Here." I offered him the little garden trowel from my backpack. "Dig with this. When you're done, leave it on that flat rock and I'll pick it up after I nymph this run."

"Uh, well, maybe I better try to make it back to the campground," he said, shifting his weight from foot to foot and visibly tightening his sphincter. "I think I'd feel better about it—you know, not polluting and all. *Giardia,* you know. Parasites. Bacteria. Viruses. We have to be responsible citizens of the planet. If you're going to spend time in the wilderness you really ought to think about things like that."

"Well, I do both, actually, but suit yourself—and take the TP just in case." I said. "And, uh, you from around here?"

"Bangor," he said.

"Lived there long?"

"I moved there from New York last year."

I watched him shuffle back upriver like a toddler with a load in his pants—a man who, like his countless ancestors before him, was about to drop his daily deposit of excess nitrogen, phosphorous, and potassium, only he wasn't about to dump it into the quiet hungry forest but into a poisonous plastic Porta-Potti that gets sucked dry weekly by a traveling honey wagon then emptied into a sewage-treatment facility built twenty years ago to handle the population of thirty years before. He was a man of strong convictions, a man who meant well but had not learned well. Just like most of us.

A few years ago Kathleen Meyer's *How to Shit in the Woods: An Environmentally Sound Approach to a Lost Art* was on *Outdoor Retailer*'s bestselling book list for months. I remember thinking at the time, Yegods, has it come to this? Can there really be people running loose in the woods who need a book to tell them how to crap?

Of course part of the book's attraction was its poo-poo ca-ca doo-doo subject matter. We Americans love tittering over toilet issues as much as we hate actually thinking about them. Imagine all those book browsers snickering over the cover—a man in the woods with his pants around his ankles, a shovel in one hand and a trailing roll of toilet paper in the other—and thinking, Now *here's* a neat little stocking stuffer for that Woodsy One on my Christmas list. That's how I got my copy: a naughty novelty, like a package of plastic puke or a pair of underpants labeled HOME OF THE WHOPPER. But unlike most naughty novelties, *How to Shit in the Woods* was genuinely useful, for there really are thousands of people waddling around out there with their pants around their ankles who don't know how to answer nature's call—at least not in a responsible manner, judging from all the paper-draped turds abandoned in plain sight.

It's all so simple. Likely it was common knowledge even before Charlton Heston wrote these explicit instructions in Deuteronomy: *Thou shalt have a place also without the camp, whither thou shalt go forth abroad: And thou shalt have a paddle upon thy weapon; and it shall be, when thou wilt ease thyself abroad, thou shall dig therewith, and shalt turn back and cover that which cometh from thee.* Thirty-two hundred years later and that's still pretty much all there is to it: Get above the high-water mark, dig a little hole in a place not too wet and not too dry, then cover up that which cometh from thee. If you have a choice, wipe your butt with indigenous vegetation, because unlike poo-poo ca-ca doo-doo, toilet paper takes its time going back to the earth. If nature calls in thick and abrasive evergreen growth, or the desert, or some other place bereft of indigenous scouring agents of acceptable texture and reproductive profligacy, I use toilet paper. And if conditions are right, I hasten the TP's return to the earth by very carefully torching it.

"How can you even take a chance on burning down the forest?" I hear various Smokies the Bear saying, shaking their fingers at a benighted rustic destructive in his ignorance. And the answer is, By noting the presence of wind and the surrounding terrain's inflammability, by knowing that organic topsoil burns but that mineral subsoil a few inches down doesn't, and by carrying a full water bottle so I can simultaneously wash up away from the river and sluice down the embers, I *don't* take a chance on burning down the forest, no more than I take a chance on polluting a wilderness stream I love with a fly fisher's self-interested passion by crapping in a well-buried cat hole twenty yards back into the puckerbrush. It's all in understanding how things work. Having lived in the country most of my life, where dealing with crap in one form or another is simply the stuff of existence, it's kind of hard *not* to know how things work.

We have existed in a more or less recognizable form for some three million years and as the species we are now for more than two hundred thousand years, but only in the past sixty or so years have we severed bonds with the earth that have existed for as long as we have been us. Only one in four people, the census bureau tells us, still lives in a rural area, the result being that strident urbanites two generations off the farm who no longer know where food comes from insist that whatever has worked for eons be stopped right now, this instant, because it offends their supermarket sensibilities.

We in the country see every day the effects of this well-meaning societal disconnect: nice-sounding laws with wide popular support that create five big problems for every small one they tried to correct;

complex regulations labored over in air-conditioned urban offices that mildly inconvenience a shit-squirting corporate hog factory and drive a fifth-generation small farmer to a dead-end factory job and his wife to secret drinking; dewy-eyed cityfolk seeking a closer walk with nature who sue the farmer next door for spreading manure on his fields at five in the morning; sanctimonious suburbanites who decree all hunting be stopped now and forevermore because death is oh-so-horrible and then demand airdrops of baited birth-control pills when deer eat their begonias and cougars their poodles; plaintive pleas from urban cowboys who wandered into the wayback with no compass, no map, no food, no water, no skills, not even any Boy Scout book learning—nothing but a mad new hunger for the well-advertised wild and a mobile phone in case of inconvenience.

Not that rural people are paragons of ecological intelligence. We have, in fact, a long history of abusing the environment that supports us: garbage dumped in anonymous back-road turnouts; old car batteries and waste oil buried in backyard bogs that directly feed springs and wells; strip-mine tillage of monocultural wastelands; no-prisoners forestry; pesticides and herbicides and high-voltage fertilizers sprayed indiscriminately and usually unnecessarily; hollow trees stuffed with dirty diapers; fly-buzzed turds decorating country paths and logs and bare rocks where returning to the soil through the digestive tracts of worms and microorganisms is less likely than an airborne invasion of your digestive tract courtesy of the fly toeing your egg-salad sandwich. All this, too, stems from ignorance, just as does the urban majority's well-intentioned proscription of country ways.

We are all bozos on this overcrowded bus, out-of-touch know-nothings the lot of us, and for this I blame indoor plumbing. With tongue only partly in cheek, I judge Thomas Crapper's most famous invention guilty, at least in part, of stuffing our collective heads tightly between our collective cheeks.

When we lost touch, so to speak, with that which cometh from us, we lost the inescapable understanding that everything in the world is interconnected, that what goes in always comes out, that everyone and everything in the world is downhill and downstream from someone and something else, that all life is an endless wheel of birth, death, and decay.

Taking a dump in the woods from time to time might do wonders for some of those cityfolk, providing they spread out and learn how it's properly done. Believe it or not, outdoor deposition can even be an aesthetic experience. A trip to the squat pit puts you outdoors with the time to think about and notice your surroundings—the chirping birds and humming mosquitoes, the worms looking forward to what's left of last night's corn and beans. It's certain, unless you're of a scatological turn of mind, that you aren't thinking about what it is you actually came here to do. Like your ancestors before you, your mind drifts far away, one of the few times of the day when you're utterly unburdened.

We would all be better humans if we did this occasionally—and again I'm saying this only partly in jest. I do indeed think an outdoor crap, or at the very least an outdoor whiz, is crucial to understanding how you as an insignificant atom fit into the cosmic whole. But if we all rushed into the woods with our pants around our ankles . . . well. To quote from Lattee Fahm's 1980 book, *The Waste of Nations: Global Prospects for Recycling Human Waste in Agriculture,* "Some 4.5 billion people produce excretal matters at about 5.5 million metric tons every twenty-four hours, close to two billion metric tons per year." Twenty years later, with our randy species nearing 7 billion individuals, that's a whole lot of cat holes dug back in the puckerbrush.

When I slouch on the couch glowering at the evening news, wondering, as all humans do, how all of this weirdness going on is going to affect me, I shake my head at just how many problems we face, and how so many of them stem directly from how many of us we have become.

As I write this, two-thirds of the way through the first year of the new millennium, the U.S. population clock is just ticking past 275 million. When I was born in 1949, 149,188,130 people admitted their existence to the U.S. Census Bureau. When my father was born in 1912, the U.S. population stood at 95,335,000.

I wonder, sitting on the couch wincing at televised images of starvation and urban strife, whether mine will be the last generation that enjoys the wild wholesale and not in premeasured and infrequent doses of unfamiliar novelty.

Where does it end? In his role as intermediary, Moses wagged his finger and said, Cover up that which cometh from thee. He also transcribed his boss's earlier command that we be fruitful and multiply, but I'm thinking the stenographer got that one wrong, or maybe the dictator was very bad at mathematics or wasn't looking very far into the future. Or perhaps He/She/It hadn't foreseen the result of the most recent biological experiment's facility for multiplication.

Thomas Malthus, in *An Essay on the Principle of Population,* wrote that "the advocate for the present order of things is apt to treat the sect of speculative philosophers either as a set of artful and designing knaves who preach up ardent benevolence and draw captivating pictures of a happier state of society only the better to enable them to destroy the present establishments and to forward their own deep-laid schemes of ambition, or as wild and mad-headed enthusiasts whose silly speculations and absurd paradoxes are not worthy of the attention of any reasonable man."

So, happy to be a mad-headed enthusiast filled with silly speculations and absurd paradoxes, I invite you into the woods to take your ease. And while you're there, trying to think about everything else but what you came here to do, look around at the contradictions of our compressing world—the constant corporate clamor for more and ever more, the gas-guzzling SUVs papered over with SAVE THE EARTH bumper stickers, the earnest young granola-crunching Greenpeace couple who spawn seven children merely because they are biologically capable of doing so—and imagine, in a hundred years, where all those people yet to come are going to crap, never mind where they'll find a clean-running wild trout stream where they can spend a solitary week listening to its music and answering nature's call.

11

Fish Willies

And the night shall be filled with music,
And the cares, that infest the day,
Shall fold their tents, like the Arabs,
And as silently steal away.

—HENRY WADSWORTH LONGFELLOW,
"The Day Is Done"

You can't really call it a phobia. I'm just not all that fond of spiders, is all. Too many close encounters with black widows brooding beneath boyhood outhouse seats awaiting sensitive things that dangle. Too many brown recluses summering in closeted coat pockets until the cool of autumn brings quivering pink hands. Too many revenant images of an enormous garden spider struggling beneath the wreckage of its web, which had shrink-wrapped to my six-year-old face as I dove through tall weeds. Too many breathless news clips about the hot-tempered European hobo spider, an unintended 1920s introduction to the Pacific Northwest that makes the flesh-sloughing brown recluse seem as sweetly benign as a Disney cartoon.

129

In early autumn on Oregon's Deschutes River, everything is spiders. Spiders along the banks. Spiders in the tents. Spiders in the sleeping bags. Spiders in waders hung out to dry. Spiders in the treetops grown gross and gouty on the river's infinite insect banquet.

Spiders just give me the willies, is all.

The Willies.

In the ballet *Giselle* the Wilis were the ghosts of jilted brides who had been left weeping at the altar with red faces and wilted bouquets. At night the shadowy white Wilis haunted the forest looking for young men, whom they'd force to dance unto death in an elegantly matrimonial tit-for-tat. These nineteenth-century balletic Wilis derive from far older Slavic water witches called Wili or Vila who danced in the moonlight, lured young men into cold rivers, and, for some unknown but probably appropriate gender-vengeful reason, drowned their sorry asses. The embedded dread of these ancient nighttime naiads survived through the centuries as a wonderfully descriptive expression for an automatic emotion that, triggered by one stimulus or another, afflicts us all.

So spiders give me the willies. And so does the dark.

Which may explain why, as half the buzzards in the Oregon desert swooped into their river-moated nest tree and the sun dipped below the harsh basaltic cliffs that stand like ruined Scottish castles all along the Lower Deschutes, I began to think about white-veiled dancers pirouetting airily through the moonlight. It helped take my mind off the spiders, a good quart of which Ted and I swept from the inflatable before dropping down to the midriver gravel bar where we hoped to do some moonlit dancing of our own with redsides trout.

The Deschutes River redsides is to a regulation rainbow what a supercharged Susquehanna smallmouth is to a slack-finned warmouth: members of the same species in the same way that a Ferrari and a Yugo are both imported automobiles. Redsides are a deep Tucson red, a slice of rare beef crusted black on the edges and heavily peppered. Their thick untapered bodies ripple with power-lifter muscles, and their fierce hard eyes glare with screw-you defiance. Until you stretch the tape you simply won't believe that the eighteen-incher you fought furiously to the forceps is only thirteen inches long.

And thirteen-inchers is what we'd caught, mostly, in a laid-back week of floating and camping and genially farting around: a couple of friends afflicted by varying degrees of middle age and unnecessarily obtrusive careers, taking time off to recharge psychic batteries with food and wine and conversation and artful indolence. And trout, of course.

Over the week there'd been a good scattering of those thirteen-inchers and a few much bigger ones, mostly dredged up inelegantly on strings of beadheads: a fifty-foot waterhaul up and across, then a long, long, slack-feeding drift as far downstream as you could see the indicator. It worked well enough in the unrelenting September sun, but it lacked drama.

Drama is what we were after on the gravel bar that night. And drama, of course, means dry flies.

It's not a purist thing at all. It's just that the sight of a good fish inhaling your cocky floating fly raises hackles in a way a twitch of the fluffy floating indicator cannot. A good rise brings an electric thrill. It gives you the willies, is what it does.

That gravel bar didn't need rising trout to give me the willies: the deep green current sweeping past its steep and readily erodable pea-gravel carapace; the scraggly gnarled willows furring its spine and anchoring it tenuously midstream; the giant upstream cottonwood alive with nattering buzzards looming ominously above the battlemented basalt in a lightning-flashed scene from a 1930s horror film;

the amorphous line of bankside trees thickly gauzed with cobwebs and skittering spiders like a chorus line of topiary Moais dressed to dance *Giselle* then dine on Miss Havisham's wedding cake. It was enough to give anyone the willies.

At least, I thought in Schwiebertian italics as I felt my way out to the edge of the drop-off, slid chest-deep, grabbed a handful of willows, scrabbled my way back onto more or less firm ground, and felt around for my fly rod, *there ain't no spiders out here.*

And no rising trout, either, as near as we could tell. We marked time tossing beadheads, each of us taking from our respective port-and-starboard seams a couple of stalwart eighteen-inch redsides that the tape unmasked as regulation thirteen-inchers; each of us losing in quick sequence a truly good fish in the tangle of willows that stitched together the stern half of this topographically restive gravel bar; each of us pretending, as dusk dwindled to dark and we bumbled through the ritual of rerigging, that our night vision and our close vision were not receding apace with our hairlines and muscle tone.

As we felt through our fly boxes for tactile inspiration, a subtle slurping drifted down on the wind, and as we knelt low to the river's dull gleam we could see, just above the knee-deep waters of the gravel bar's leading edge, clouds of tiny black caddisflies dancing through the gloaming, zigging and zagging and dipping to the water to lay eggs, and occasionally to be met by open jaws.

So we bit off the beadheads we had laboriously tied on and fumbled through boxes, glasses pushed back on anxious brows, bare eyeballs skimming at Elk Hair level for anything that looked like a tiny dark caddis. We poked furiously at hook eyes like dimestore sewing machines, eventually and purely accidentally threading tippets through eyes, then wrapping the five and a half turns and back through the loop, and wetting the turns and cinching them down then wiping wings and hackle with a thin film of flotant, as all the while tiny black caddisflies zigged and zagged beneath our noses and across our faces and not fifteen feet away wrought-iron snouts split hard pewter water and slurped and sipped and cut hungry ponderous V-wakes with broad muscular backs.

We cast then, finally, sidearming curves into the current's slack edges, and we struck at rises we imagined were near our flies and on rare occasions were, and then we'd connect with a throbbing angry weight that would tear downstream and upstream and across the stream and into the air, all the while shaking and dogging his head, trying to tear away this thing that had him by the jaw, this thing that would not let go, at least not willingly, at least not until we could bring him in and turn him upside down in the curling dark water and tweeze the fly from his jaws, and admire his strength and supple beauty there in the last flicker of twilight, and let him go and feel the leader for nicks, then scramble to rerig and retie and cast once again before it all became more futile than it already was.

We caught more eighteen-inchers that were thirteen-inchers, and a couple of two-footers that *were* eighteen inchers, and at least two three-footers that taped an honest twenty, and we were both broken off, once again and irrevocably, by huge solid weights that had taken our little Elk Hairs like orcas take a seal, there not fifteen feet away from our staggering middle-aged knees in the watching night, weights that had bored for the bottom and raced downstream and tangled us, each of us separately and each of us together, in the twisted knee-high willows that alone gave this gravel bar a shape and a life.

And finally night and mature judgment won out over boyish optimism and denial, and as Ted sloshed along the bank toward camp dragging the inflatable and I trudged along a twisting formless bankside trail grown over with thorns and puncture grass and rattlesnakes and whatever else malignant and mean this inhospitable land could devise to thwart humanity's inexorable tide, I could see, backlit against the stars, clouds of tiny black caddisflies dancing above the treetops and into the thick silvery cobwebs that bid them to a banquet, while out in the black river faint slurps still sounded, and high overhead came the sibilant snackering of hungry little fangs.

It was enough to give you the willies.

12

Little Jewels

*Finally from the crease of the ravine I am follow-
ing there begins to come the trickling and splashing of water. There is a great restfulness in the
sounds these small streams make; they are going
down as fast as they can, but their sounds seem
leisurely and idle, as if produced like gemstones
with the greatest patience and care.*

—WENDELL BERRY,
"An Entrance to the Woods"

This brook has a name, but I don't know you well enough to
tell you what it is. You probably wouldn't care anyway: It's just
an unimposing thread of thin tannic water splitting a blue-green forest flecked with autumn's crimson and gold, a little slip of a stream
skipping unnoticed down a mountainside toward a marriage with a
big Maine river famous for its fishing. And because this is a crisp
puffy-cumulus Sunday within twenty-four hours of season's end, that
river is crowded with fly fishers drawn there by crowds of trout and

salmon—the prespawn runup to biological raison d'être for the fish, the last frenetic licks at a too-short season for the fishers.

Although it's the end of my too-short season, too, I've ducked out after a few days of frenzy and gone off alone a voyeur, for up this brook the *pre-* no longer prefaces the *spawn,* and brook trout are building redds wherever flowing water aerates pea gravel. I've brought no rod, of course, and wouldn't have even if the season on brooks and streams hadn't already closed. It's bad enough bothering fish when they're merely eyeing each other hopefully; bothering them after they've hooked up and are enthusiastically perpetuating their species is inexcusable. Besides, I need some space from fishing this year to think about the fishing this year, along with some other things that want sorting out, and I've brought only a notebook, a pen, a lunch, and the aquatic Peeping Tom's essential duo of binoculars and polarized glasses.

I brought along something else, too: a piece of music that started playing in my head on a train ride from Devon to Scotland back in June and hasn't stopped since. You know how it happens. One minute you're innocently brushing your teeth, and the next you're humming You'll Wonder Where the Yellow Went When You Brush Your Teeth with Pepsodent. Attack music like this tends to drone on forever until chased out by another song. If you're lucky it'll be something by Pink Floyd or B. B. King or Bach or whoever it is that twists your dial; if you aren't lucky it'll be "We Welcome You to Munchkin Land" or the theme from Petticoat Junction—*Here's Unca Joe, he's a-movin' kinda slow, at da junkshun.* Over and over and over again.

But the piece of music I'm trying to get rid of is one I've always loved, or I did before it became as persistent this summer as the ache from my brand-new arthritis. It came to haunt me before, and when it did, the only thing that could chase it away was this little brook; bursting like trumpets down the mountainside, it can drown out nearly anything, even the dull ache of lost love and the mournful march from Henry Purcell's *Funeral Music for Queen Mary*.

The music that buried Queen Mary and, less than a year later, Purcell himself, provided an appropriate soundtrack for burying the last remnants of what I had thought back then was my life. This summer, after nearly thirty years of unexpected happiness, it came back to mourn the sharp pangs of manifest middle age and what poet Sir John Betjeman called "late-blooming lust." As any middle-aged male will tell you, the two often travel together.

The brook winds down through a natural amphitheater filled with La-Z-Boy boulders upholstered with thick green moss, providing pleasant fishing as the brook dodges and weaves past and pleasant platforms for lounging around, listening to the natural music of fast-moving water, and idly watching trout fuck.

Trout go about it so predictably, as, I suppose, do we. It begins with a wink and a nod, a sympathetic connection between two members of the same species who see one another and like what they see. Whether this is chemical, electrical, or cosmic in nature, no one knows.

It just happens: A glance. A smile. A wriggle. *Zap*. Or as Beavis and Butthead would say, *Boyoyoyoyoyoing*.

Next thing you know a nursery's under construction, with the female doing all the work and the male puffing out his rib cage and looking all pleased with himself, and then after a quick spasm and a spurt or two he's off bragging to his buds and chasing another set of soft waving fins.

Folks who say animals and humans have nothing in common beyond chemical composition haven't spent much time watching either.

Not long after I came back from Britain I was fishing up the South Fork of Colorado's Frying Pan, the remote stretch that runs between the willowy flat water where it joins the Middle Fork and the stair step falls that lift it high into the mountains. Industrious beavers had dammed chains of ponds separated by quick pocket water and small plunge pools. Every pocket held a brook trout, every pool a brown. It didn't matter, really, what fly I used, so long as it was small and floated and hit the right spot.

The beaver ponds predictably held better fish, but they were much harder to catch. I flushed twenty trout for every one I caught and probably flushed twenty more I never saw. When I did everything right—meaning glacially and furtively—I tied into some serious fish for a stream only a few rod lengths wide: half a dozen brookies in the fifteen-inch range and one fat boy that taped an honest seventeen, his bulging belly all pumpkin orange and the overstated vermiculations across his broad green back wriggling like a hula girl tattooed on a bosun's biceps. Then there were the browns—such a drab name for such a colorful fish: deep yellows sprinkled with sharp reds and electric blues—seemingly every color *but* brown. Four of these high-mountain browns were around sixteen inches, and one measured exactly eighteen and five-eighths inches from nose to tail, Velveeta yellow and fat as a Rotarian.

The biggest brown and the biggest brookie both came from the same deep skirling run at the head of a beaver pond. An old gauging station cantilevered out over the deepest hole, and beneath it small cream duns disappeared in rhythmic rings.

I needed five tries at a left-curving sidearm roll cast before I finally got a fly in there, and the big brown took it as freely as a hatchery rainbow sips a kibble. The big brookie came a half dozen feet up the bank, just where a draping tussock said he should be.

Around the next bend, deep beneath an overhang stitched together by aspen roots, I saw the flick of a tail and sat down to watch. After a while I could just make out a big fish tucked up under the bank. He seemed to be feeding, but on what I couldn't tell. Grasshoppers were hopping, so I floated a Dave's Hopper past his hole a dozen times. Nothing. I crimped on a splitshot then sent the hopper drifting by at his eye level, twitching it like a lost soul reaching for the lifeline. Nothing. I tried him from downstream, upstream, across the stream. Nothing. I tried Muddlers, Woolly Buggers, stonefly nymphs, even a deer-hair mouse left over from a trip to Labrador. Nothing.

I set down my rod, hunted up some live hoppers, and drifted them down one at a time. Nothing. Then I picked at a rotting log half in and half out of the water and found some thumb-thick white grubs, and from twenty feet upstream I sent one tumbling his way. It disappeared in a wink of white mouth. I sent another after it, and he took that one too.

Trout are mostly pattern feeders, focusing on one thing that in some way fires their rockets while ignoring everything else. Who knows what it will be? Usually it's the food available in the largest quantity at a given time, but it can be anything, for as I've found from seven years of watching the goings-on in my backyard pond, trout are as much individuals as dogs, cats, or people—targeting, perhaps, crayfish or tadpoles or who knows what to the exclusion of everything else. Once you figure out the pattern, you can catch nearly any trout you can watch long enough to find out what trips his personal trigger.

The closest thing in my fly box to a grub was a big cream rabbit-fur leech, which I barbered a bit and sent drifting down the same path as the real grubs, over and over again. And nothing.

There was one grub left, and I considered sending it down with a hook inside, for by now I'd gotten a good look at the trout, a hook-jawed old brown close to two feet long. Finally I decided if I couldn't catch him my way, meaning on a fly and not live bait, I'd rather not catch him at all, so I tossed in the last grub and he snarfed it like a popover hot from the oven. With the sun just touching the mountains, I headed back.

That night I sat talking with the other folks at camp. They'd fished down below the dam and had caught some of those giant Frying Pan trout that inflate like zeppelins on *Mices* shrimp and tiny ephemera, and from thirty feet away can tell who tied your fly and what brand of 7X tippet you're using. They asked where I'd gone and how I'd done. I told them I'd gone up the Upper Frying Pan and by my standards had done well. I hadn't seen another human and had seen elk and rabbits and eagles and a coyote and blue skies and green trees, and I'd caught lots of pretty fish that weren't very bright and a couple of big ones that were a bit more challenging, and I'd spent an interesting hour or so trying unsuccessfully for a real monster I knew I could have caught if I'd been willing to ignore my self-imposed barrier between right and wrong, which I wasn't. In short, I said, I'd had a perfect day.

And it almost was, you know. Except that on the three-mile hike back to the parking lot I had to keep sitting down to rest, my knees wobbling and my lungs as saggy as yesterday's birthday balloons. I didn't tell them about that. And I didn't tell them about my self-righteous pride in, to twist a line from H. L. Mencken, being the kind of person who does the right thing even when no one is looking, because I was no longer sure I was really that kind of person at all. And I didn't tell them about hearing the music of Henry Purcell in the riffles and seeing fey green eyes swirling in the pools, either, because I knew they wouldn't have understood. But because people have come to expect it of me I did tell them a couple of East Tennessee stories I'd picked up on a visit home back in May. I'd picked up the first shudder of my Big Chill down there, too, but I didn't tell them about that, either. When in doubt, stick to safe ground.

    ᖇ ᖇ ᖇ ᖇ ᖇ ᖇ

Before it was overwhelmed by Knoxville's lava-flow growth, Lenoir City had a reputation for small-town craziness notable even for East Tennessee, where small-town craziness is an art form. Lenoir City stories could go on for hours. We were staying at my brother's cabin in Tellico, and in the evenings Jim-Bob and Walter and I would take turns telling them to Steve, a native of East Tennessee though from a more genteel part. He'd just shake his head and groan and swear we were making them up, but no one can make up stories like those.

Steve's theory is, there was a train wreck thereabouts and the survivors—a troupe of baggy-pants vaudevillians, a traveling opera company, and a cluster of escapees from an insane asylum—settled down and intermarried. He's wrong, of course. Lenoir City was actually a planned industrial community thrown together by a consortium of New York investors who snapped up dead plantations cheap in the economic aftermath of the War Between the States, laid out a small but regimented grid of streets imaginatively named First Avenue and B Street, built a railway car manufactory and a couple of cotton mills, and invited the surrounding countryside to leave behind the mule and the plow and come die of Brown Lung. I like Steve's story better, though. Even though it isn't true, it helps explain how a wide spot in the road might have produced all those wild-eyed hillbillies who grew up as familiar with Handel and Purcell and Sibelius and Tchaikovsky as we were with Homer and Jethro and Flatt and Scruggs and crazy hermits who lived in old cars and were named after their birth defects.

One night Walter came up with a story I hadn't heard. It seems that years ago our uncle Burt and his friends were up in Knoxville riding around and drinking, four or five high school kids slumped in the back of an old open touring car, their big bare feet hung out over the doors. As they turned off Kingston Pike, Uncle Burt saw someone on the sidewalk point at them and say to his friends, "*Lee*-nore City, by God."

Then Jim-Bob came up with a new story about popular local character Lambseye Dailey. It seems that not long after I left for the navy Lambseye had gotten a job digging graves for the Click Brothers, who had bought out their former employer and gone into the mortuary business for themselves. Lambseye, figuring he'd help dig up business, had his pickup-truck doors lettered with a suitable advertising slogan:

> *If your Heart don't Tick call Click,*
> *And Here'll come Lambseye with a Shovel and a Pick.*

Steve just shook his head and groaned, *"No, no, no; no more stories about these lunatics."* Which was fine in my book, because sooner or later those lunatic stories might have gotten around to another local lunatic. Me.

The next morning I headed up the North Fork of Citico Creek with Jim-Bob. Before last night's storytelling session, I hadn't seen him since my last days in what was then one of the South's best high school bands. He was sitting over in the trombone section sawing through the low-brass underpinnings of Henry Purcell's Trumpet Voluntary—okay, it wasn't really written by Purcell but by someone called Jeremiah Clarke, and its real name is "Prince of Denmark March," but due to some sloppy historical research most people think it's called Purcell's Trumpet Voluntary, including the folks who published the sheet music we were using, and who am I to correct them?

I was sitting over in the trumpet section, a couple of spots down from first chair, blatting away at the countermelody as Sandy Hair piped off those ringing high notes. I'd practiced those notes myself since I could pick up a trumpet, Purcell's purloined piece being a trumpet player's benchmark of sorts, but in the past few years my trumpet playing had slipped, along with my grades and everything else, including my grip on reality. You could blame drinking and depression and frustration with small-town life and just about have the picture, but if you dug a little deeper you'd come up with girl trouble. It's always girl trouble, isn't it?

Above the third crossing Jim and I split up, waded into the creek a half mile apart, and started fishing. The creek hadn't changed much since that time I'd fished it some thirty-five years ago, just after I'd dropped out of school and was about to head off for the navy with bleary eyes, a heavy heart, and a hangover. Then as now there were plenty of trout, though nothing big, and then as now a dry-fly-and-nymph combo would get nailed alongside almost every rock. This isn't heroic fishing for big smart trout on classic waters. Like the Upper Frying Pan and countless thousands of similarly inconsequential streams, the North Fork is just a good place to listen to the water's wild song and effortlessly catch wild fish in the midst of beauty. They're gleaming little jewels, these little nothing streams, places where you learn to fish or remember why you fish, or lose yourself or find yourself, whichever is your pleasure.

On the way back down the trail—a couple of newly middle-aged men puffing and wheezing with the day's exertions and more than a little surprised to find how decrepit we'd gotten—we started talking about old times, as former classmates who haven't seen each other in more than three decades tend to do. Catching up on old friends from school days, you know?

We ran down the list of this one and that one: this one becoming a surgeon and that one a long-haul truck driver; this one selling cars and that one gone off a monkey trainer with the circus of all things; this one teaching school and that one doing time; this one dying of a heart attack and that one in Vietnam. Finally I asked Jimmy about . . .

hmmmmm, what name should I use? Let's just stick to pronouns. Jim-Bob said he hadn't seen her for a while. He said she turned up in town from time to time and hadn't turned out well, rattling off a list of common modern-day sins. I clucked my tongue and said, Yes, I'd heard about that, and wasn't it awful. I hadn't thought about her for years, I said.

Hadn't thought about her for years . . .

She was a long-legged green-eyed brunette, with a tender little overbite and high breasts the size and shape of halved oranges. Sweat ten pounds off Neve Campbell and stretch her half a foot taller and you'll just about have the picture. We'd known each other when we were little kids living a year and a half and a quarter mile apart, but we'd lost touch when her family moved out to the country and didn't meet again until junior high. I saw her across the room at a friend's house and didn't know who she was, though she knew me. *Wow*, I said when the name finally registered on the face. You sure grew up. *Wow.*

A glance. A smile. A wriggle. *Zap.*

We had been An Item, sharing our first kiss and our first furtive fondlings on a church hayride, and although I was only briefly her item she never stopped being mine. She sat over in the woodwind section those last days of band practice, trying not to notice how I never stopped staring her way with sad puppy-dog eyes—had not, in fact, stopped staring her way with sad puppy-dog eyes since she'd said the cruelest words a lovesick teenager can hear: "I love you to bits, but as a friend."

She'd said she wanted us always to be friends, that her life wasn't going well, that things were tough at home and she *needed* my friendship. But in the all-or-nothing absolutism of the teenage male, I rejected eternal friendship and held out for Romeo-and-Juliet Love. To win back what I had so briefly held I tried all sorts of desperate and unsuccessful strategies—kindling jealousy, becoming a *West Side Story* caricature of a hoodlum—and through my efforts became something of a school joke, a skinny unrealistic romantic driven mad by love.

She'd be turning fifty in a few months, and I hadn't seen her in thirty-five years. Imagine that.

The first time I fished my way up this little Maine brook my first marriage was coming apart. It started coming apart almost as soon as it went together, though it took me three years to notice. She was a long-legged green-eyed brunette, with a tender little overbite and high breasts the size and shape of halved oranges. Imagine Gelsey Kirkland dancing Clara in the *Nutcracker,* add not quite enough Minnie Driver and a bit too much Cher, and you'll just about have the picture.

We met in Boston as friends of friends, and re-met at the old Berkeley Street Tea Party for Led Zeppelin's first American concert, just after they'd stopped being the lame-o New Yardbirds and before they became an overblown caricature of themselves. We bumped into each other in the crowd, just as Jimmy Page ripped a riff off the neck of his Les Paul and sprayed us both with sweat—a hormonal baptism of sorts.

A glance. A smile. A wriggle. *Zap. Boyoyoyoyoying.*

I believed our hearts and other organs had melded into one eternal pump, but over time my heart became an artifact collecting frost in the freezer, along with a slice of stale wedding cake and her first toe shoes. I kept telling myself it wasn't really happening, which of course means it was.

After things finally came apart, I moved to Maine and spent my weekends wading through sweet little trout streams and my nights alone in a shack in the Maine woods wading through Purcell's

Funeral Music for Queen Mary, picking out the brass-quartet march as chords on my beat-up old Telecaster and playing floorboard timpani with my feet. Over and over and over again.

I'd first heard it performed by my dad's choir back in East Tennessee, about the same time I first heard the love of my life say, "We should just be friends." I next heard it performed at a concert in Boston, the same night the new love of my life said, "I won't be moving with you to Maine."

And then one day in a Bangor camera store I met a blue-eyed blonde—modernize Veronica Lake with a big stir of Gwyneth Paltrow and weird things up with Dorothy Parker playing *I Love Lucy,* and you'll just about have the picture.

A glance. A smile. And a wriggle and a zap, though tinged less with the brooding Brontëan passion I believed to be True Love than with the easy familiarity, house-slipper comfort, and genuine affection of lifelong friendship. After some initial bobbing and weaving, my life went from wild mood swings to twenty-seven years of cozy contentment—less Heathcliff and Cathy embracing on the moors than two ten-year-olds in a treehouse tossing water balloons on passersby. Endless fun. Endless happiness.

Who'd even think of screwing up something like that?

My friends down on the river don't understand how I can think of trading the last few hours of the season on one of Maine's best trout and salmon rivers for a day of poking around a dinky little brook. They could almost understand it if I was up here fishing—although they don't share my fetish for little fish in small streams they at least respect a genuine obsession when they see one. But today I've chosen not to fish at a time when of all times I should be fishing. They don't get that at all. I didn't really try to explain, any more than I'd tried to explain this business with Henry Purcell.

Purcell was a prodigy, a composer ahead of his times, and the perfect person to score a misty-eyed nostalgic's autumnal years, for his specialty was "wistfulness and melancholy," as any number of conspicuously academic liner notes will tell you. The captive music man for Charles II, James II, and William and Mary, a writer of everything from court welcome songs and soaring church music to Top Forty show tunes, he died at the age of thirty-six from pneumonia he got after his wife locked him out of the house one cold and bitter night.

No one knows how he pissed her off, though if you read some of his show-tune lyrics you can hazard a guess:

> *I gave her Cakes and I gave her Ale,*
> *And I gave her Sack and sherry,*
> *I kist her once and I kist her twice,*
> *and we were wond'rous merry.*
> *I gave her Beads and bracelets fine,*
> *And I gave her Gold down derry,*
> *I thought she was afear'd till she stroak'd my Beard,*
> *and we were wond'rous merry.*

Purcell was fifteen years younger than me when he died. My father died at sixty-two, eleven years older than I am now. Queen Mary wasn't quite thirty-four.

After years of joking about getting old, this year I finally felt the chill of oncoming winter. Suddenly I'm *Mature*, damn it. And maturity, I have found, has less to do with discovering such universal truths as the brevity of childhood and life in general than with discovering they actually apply to you. Like most baby boomers, I'd thought myself immune not only to aging but also to the idiocy aging can cause, the stupid, stupid things we do as we clutch at vanishing youth.

Hookup time in Maine: A brook trout hen about eleven inches long has begun digging a pocket for her eggs. A tubby old male crowding sixteen inches is hovering around looking flamboyant and self-satisfied. She's flexing her tail powerfully, fluttering gravel up into the current and downstream. Soon she has a depression the size of a custard cup, and she vibrates like a tuning fork as she extrudes a string of eggs. The big male is rubbing along her side and spewing milt in ecstatic spurts, then he darts quickly around the pool, the piscean equivalent of going all high-fives and *Yes*, I'm one helluva *man*. But the female has already moved just upstream and is digging another pocket, and as she begins to vibrate and lay eggs and the big male comes swaggering up swinging his watch chain and slicking back his pompadour, a little weasel of a trout about eight inches long jets from behind a rock and ejaculates teenage milt all over the place. So happy is he to be him, the big male doesn't at first notice he's just been hung with a cuckold's horns, and when he does he lumbers off after his rival in full afterburner retreat. You want to say, Serves him right, the self-satisfied old hound. But then you notice his frayed fins and the trace of fungus behind his gills, and you realize this might be his last trip to the spawning grounds, and you know just how he feels. At least you do if you're a middle-aged male who's just realized reality applies to you, too.

I had been touring the minor chalkstreams of southwest England for much of June, couch-surfing from friend to friend and fishing here and there through scattered bits of private water where friends and friends of friends had permission to trespass.

I was staying with Birch near Salisbury for a few days. We had fished in the morning and at noon were headed for a pub on the

Avon to meet his girlfriend, who was coming down from London with some friends for a weekend in the country. After lunch we'd give them fly-fishing lessons, Birch said, sounding not exactly thrilled but being a grudging good sport about it, like the good Oxbridge boy he is.

But they weren't really interested in fly fishing, that crowd. They were just interested in lolling around the Avon's cowslip banks, drinking champagne and talking about the things Town People talk about whether they're in town or country, which is basically how dumb everyone is but them.

Birch headed off upstream with fly rod in hand and two tipsy Townies in tow. I wandered downstream with a woman who hadn't gotten bombed on champagne and begun parroting prefabricated platitudes, like the others, and had laughed long and loud at my obscure snide asides, unlike the others. She was tall and pale and wore blue jeans and a T-shirt, with a baseball cap hiding tightly braided dark hair and small sunglasses with blue-and-white gingham frames hiding her eyes.

She seemed nominally connected to an annoying nasal Aussie, a doughy dickhead with a Porsche who, through an undemanding life lived on Daddy's money, fancied himself a smashing dude and a right-clever smartass.

"Ever fly fished before?" I asked her as we turned to look at the stream.

"No," she said. "But it looks so beautiful, like poetry or dance."

"Good answer. We were introduced back at the pub. I got your friend's name but I've forgotten yours."

"M'reese," she said.

"Say again? Mau-reese?"

"No. M-a-u-r-y-c-e. Clip the first syllable and breath into the second syllable. Mu-*rees*. It's an old family name. And you are?"

"Babb. James Babb. My friends call me Jim."

"Shaken not stirred, right?" She laughed and hummed a bit of James Bond, then said, "He's not my friend."

"The Aussie?"

"He's Patsy's husband's friend, not mine. Patsy thought a weekend in the country might be good for me, and I caught a ride down from London with him. But I'm going back on the train. He drives like an idiot."

"He *is* an idiot."

"Right," she said, laughing. "He is."

We didn't catch any fish, Mauryce and I; a bright sunny day on a tough English chalkstream is not the place to learn how to catch fish. But we caught something else, when we took a break from casting lessons and she took off her sunglasses to blow her hay-fevery nose with the handkerchief she kept borrowing and I finally insisted she keep. She tossed back her hat and shook out those tight librarian braids, and with the English sun glowing orange through a cloud of shoulder-length dark hair I saw what I had not seen before, or if I had seen hadn't really noticed, in the way of folks who travel a lot and briefly meet lots of people they never expect to see again. She was a long-legged green-eyed brunette, with a tender little overbite and high breasts the size and shape of halved oranges. Mix equal parts Audrey Hepburn and Christy Turlington, sprinkle lightly with Penélope Cruz and Catherine Zeta-Jones, and you'll just about have the picture.

A glance. A smile . . .

Birch and I were supposed to swap off teaching the various Townies to cast, but Mauryce and I moved downstream around the bend from their party, unwilling to share our own.

We talked and we talked and we talked, while all the while the fly line rolled and unrolled like an acrobat's streamer in a May Day parade. We talked of our childhoods, our lives, our loves, our aspirations. She was a writer, too, as it turned out, and had just finished her first book—an academic inquiry into the parallels between the nineteenth-century German and Russian mental-health systems that she was thinking of reworking into a book for real people to read and enjoy and not just for academia nuts to tear apart and reconstruct into their own careers. We talked, as writers do, of the things we wanted to say and the things we hoped to make people see, of words and sentences and paragraphs arranged and rearranged then rearranged again—the windy vain shop talk, as J. B. Priestley wrote, of those "who do little tricks with words and pigments and fiddle strings."

It was while finishing her book that she knew she was meant to be a real writer, she said, and not a career academic who published only to avoid professionally perishing. And as she began reworking her book into a completely new form she found she would have to completely rework her life, too, for as it turned out her storybook marriage where hearts intertwined in everlasting love had in fact been a phantom construct—her warm beating heart, so unreservedly given as a wedding gift seven years before, had been but a trifling artifact kept in the fridge with the mayonnaise and marmalade.

I told her about how my own heart had once lived in cold storage without my knowing it until it was almost too far gone to thaw; how I had once been only a passing fancy, an accident of runaway hormones, a regretted impulse like a tail-wagging puppy brought home from the pound and petted and fawned over then set out for curbside pickup when it chewed the carpets and piddled on the Capezios. And we looked into each other's watery red eyes and smiled.

A glance. A smile. A wriggle . . .

∽   ∽   ∽   ∽   ∽   ∽

Birch and I were heading that evening for a friend's cow pasture, where a few hundred yards of tiny wild chalkstream flowed in tranquil splendor and the descendants of trout Walton and Cotton had likely caught rose freely through the weeds to the mayfly. Birch was driving like a maniac down a narrow twisting lane and talking a mile a minute.

"Man, I'm glad to get rid of those grotty wankers. They could have stayed in London and gotten drunk. Why bother to come out here?"

"Cityfolk," I said. "They think the countryside's their own private Disneyland. They're the voting majority, you know. In a few years they'll kill off hunting and then they'll go after fishing, all the while eating factory-farmed salmon and congratulating themselves for saving the earth."

"Bloody wankers. But that what's-her-name—the professor? She's different. You and her really hit it off, eh?"

"She's a writer, too, and having a rough time with a marriage that's coming apart the same way mine did almost thirty years ago. Right now she needs a friend who understands, I think. She said I should come see her in London."

"*Yeah?* Man, she doesn't need a friend. She needs somebody to screw her eyeballs out. Divorce? She's *vulnerable* now. If you don't go after her *you're* a bloody wanker."

"I've been happily married to the same woman for twenty-seven years and I don't intend to screw it up."

"Don't be an asshole. You're over here, your wife's over there. And I saw you two saying good-bye. Go for it."

"Piss off, Birchie. She's a nice woman in rough straits. She needs a friend, not a predator."

"Friend my ass. You go after her or I will."

He saw my face go red, and then he said, "Christ. You're in *love* with her. You sad pathetic bastard."

Right on both counts.

∾   ∾   ∾   ∾   ∾   ∾

The good-bye had started awkwardly, the way they do: the perfunctory hand clasp, the perfunctory hug, the exchange of business cards and greeting-card sentiments: *It Was So Much Fun! I Had Such a Great Time!* But then the hug didn't stop, and I looked into her eyes so close, so huge and warm and green, swirling like kaleidoscopes, the eyes of an elf queen straight out of Tolkien.

"I *really* enjoyed meeting you," she said. "I really did. If you want a break from fishing and couch-surfing Hardy country, why not surf up to London for a few days? I'd love to have you come dent my couch."

A glance. A smile. A wriggle. *Zap.*

Was there a kiss? Maybe. I don't know, really. The Avon could have burst into flames and I wouldn't have noticed. We hugged again and said it again, this time in unison, "I'm *really* glad I met you."

Did I mention all this happened on my fifty-first birthday?

Boyoyoyoyoyoing.

Somehow I'd expected my fiftieth to be the shaker and quaker, but it was just another wild June on the banks of the Penobscot with the usual suspects—raucous fun in familiar territory with familiar friends.

The fifty-first came on the banks of the faraway Avon in the company of a bunch of cityfolk I didn't want to know and a woman eighteen years my junior whom I very much did—a woman who was more than an instant friend; she fit the *pattern,* God help me.

For the next couple of weeks I fished around southwest England and Wales in a kind of daze, seeing those swirling green eyes in the water, in the trees, in the flowers, and most especially in the dark when I was alone at night and trying to sort out the difference between right and wrong, between the reality of the innocent offer of genuine friendship I knew the invitation must be and the delusional grasping at vanishing youth I was trying not to let it become.

I sent my wife a noncommittal postcard written inside a miniature medieval church in a tiny Devon hamlet where generations of my ancestors lay moldering beneath the nave:

Hi, Miss You.
Luggage lost three days. Had to buy racy English underwear.
Lots of Fun. Lots of fish. Lots of rain. Lots of dead Babbs.
Made some good friends.
Home in a few weeks.
Love you.

And then the day came when I had to begin heading north for Scotland to write the magazine article that had actually brought me over here, and after two weeks of agonizing about how the game of life is played and what the definition of honor is, I pulled out a rumpled card and dialed the phone. While it was ringing and ringing and ringing and ringing, my friend Mike's wife was running off a copy of John Eliot Gardiner's new recording of Purcell's *Funeral Music for Queen Mary* I'd heard the night before and admired.

Linda picked me up at the airport and began relating a month of accumulated news about the garden, the cats, our friends, our son out in Oregon, the weird stuff she'd seen around town or on the tube. And then she began asking about the trip—where had I gone, had I had a good time, how was the train ride to Scotland, how was the fishing, did I bring her a present?

And I said I'd couch-surfed around Wessex and Wales and had a good time, and the train ride from Devon to Scotland was long and smoky because I'd accidentally gotten aboard the smoking car and hadn't realized it until two stations up the line when the train filled with muddy dazed concertgoers from the Glastonbury Music Festival, and I'd had to sit there coughing for twelve hours alongside a chain-smoking Lancashire girl with a painted face and platinum mall hair who kept barking *Hay? Hay?* into her pink-flowered mobile phone and whining over and over, *Oi dunno whur oi yaaaaaam. Oi doon zee noothink but blooody cows an' blooody treeeeeeeeees.*

I said I'd caught some fish though as usual the weather had been intermittently nasty, and I'd brought her a bagful of strange English chocolates from the duty-free at Heathrow, having walked all over Edinburgh for two days trying unsuccessfully to find her something more interesting than a factory-made kilt for £50 more than the handmade one I'd brought her back from Braemar a few years before.

And she asked what I was doing in Edinburgh, and I said I'd gone there because I'd run out of complimentary couches in Wessex three days before I was scheduled to arrive at the lodge in Scotland, and I had meant to go up to London for a few days and stay with a new friend I'd met on the Avon, but she hadn't been home when I'd called so I'd had to go somewhere, and Edinburgh was at least on the way to northwest Sutherland and was by all accounts worth seeing.

She asked what Edinburgh was like, and I said it was architecturally unspoiled but overrun with German tourists wearing oiled hiking boots and clomping down the wrong side of the sidewalk grimly searching for souvenirs, and that with all the German tourists in town and my enormous portmanteau filled with fishing impedimenta restricting me to within a twenty-minute trundle of the train station I'd had to stay in a pricey hotel with chocolates on the pillows and unrecognizable plumbing fixtures, including what seemed to be a drinking fountain you could only drink from by kneeling, which got the you're-such-a-dumbass laugh I'd been angling for.

Having said pretty much all there was to say we drove along in silence, or at least what I'd thought was silence. Finally she asked what it was I kept humming, and I told her it was the march from Purcell's

Funeral Music for Queen Mary, that I'd been humming it since I boarded the train for Scotland and hadn't, as far as I knew, stopped for one minute since, including when I was asleep.

And then she asked what she was like, the woman whose London couch I'd hoped to surf but hadn't.

You can't keep secrets from someone you've been married to for twenty-seven years, someone who has seen the best and the worst of most of your life and knows you better than anyone else ever could. How could you even try?

I said she was really nice—a real person, you know? Someone we'd actually be friends with—smart, sarcastic, funny, compassionate, perceptive. She's a writer, too, I said, and she's just finished her first book and is thinking of another and is a compulsive rewriter like me, and she's in the midst of a sad divorce and feeling really lonely and hollow and has a nice flat in London and is looking forward to rebuilding her life and she's some kind of international expert on nineteenth-century asylums and speaks Russian and German and likes Halloween and bats and fried chicken and Lindy Hopping and she has hay fever and one of my handkerchiefs and you wouldn't believe how quickly she learned to cast a fly and . . .

"Wait. Don't tell me. She's a tall skinny brunette with cupcake tits and green eyes and a face full of teeth. Right?"

See what I mean?

Seeing the behavior and motivations of humans in the behavior and motivations of animals is called anthropomorphism. Understandably, it's widely discredited by dogmatists who mistake ancient tales for direct dictation, by hunters and agriculturalists of a certain stripe who feel admitting that animals are individuals with personalities makes killing and eating them seem too icky, and, of course, by academics driven by who-knows-what motivations to scientifically wipe those smiles off everyone's faces.

Fish don't have facial muscles, and so scientists tell us their faces can't register emotion, though anyone who has ever released a small trout and seen the terror and panic in his eyes or duped a big old cannibal brown with a slow-rolled streamer and seen rage and dismay burn like a brushfire across his face can tell you those scientists need to do more fieldwork.

They should join me here on this little Maine stream, and have a look at that tubby old trout hanging there in the current. What I see on his face isn't so much rage or dismay as resignation, a kind of cellular understanding that the jig is up and things will never be the same. I wonder if he hears music, too?

Middle-aged men and their metamorphoses . . . I'd think it was the funniest thing in the world if it wasn't happening to me. Even happening to me, it's pretty damn funny. Lucky for me, my wife thinks it's funny, too.

I've sat here watching these randy brook trout so long it's just about gone dark, and given the choice between stumbling through a couple of miles of spruce bog and spending the night with no sleeping bag I'm definitely going for the latter. I've got a fleece pullover and a rain jacket and waders, and matches and a coffeepot and some coffee, and it's not too cold and there's plenty of dry downed wood for a fire. And Linda isn't expecting me back until tomorrow or the next day, anyway, so why rush? We both enjoy our time alone nearly as much as we enjoy our time together, the one keeping the other fresh and entertaining.

Besides, it's comforting sitting alone here in the night. Even with the brook roaring I can still hear the slow plod of Purcell's march and then right through the whole suite, the three choral pieces beginning with "Man That Is Born of a Woman" hath but a short time to live, and ending with "Thou Knowest, Lord," the secrets of our hearts. Appropriate choices, those.

Like most human beings, Purcell was a contradiction, an apparent rake and rapscallion and at the same time a spinner of sacred songs that soar across the centuries. A person who genuinely wanted to do right for the sake of doing right but was biologically disposed to do wrong. Like most of us.

I could have worse background music, I suppose, as I sit here beside this brook looking into the fire, seeing green eyes and blue eyes, feeling regret and relief, thinking about emails from England and the patterns of life, and hearing those weirdly dissonant harmonies that can lift the hair right off the top of your head. And I could be doing worse things than sitting here beside a brook through a long, lonely night, stringing together a small cache of memories like little jewels, some pale and gleaming and some dark and sad, but all parts of a whole I'll take out and fondle in the not-too-distant winter of my years, reminding me there was once an autumn, and a summer and a spring.

There could be worse background music than the wild harmonies of Henry Purcell blended with wild flowing water to soundtrack the long lonely night of a middle-aged man who tried to fail and didn't, who's glad he didn't and sad he didn't and unsure of the damage he's done.

I could be hearing Jethro Tull's "Aqualung."

Fourth Movement

Winter

Winter is icummen in,
Lhude sing Goddumm,
Raineth drop and staineth slop,
And how the wind doth ramm!
Sing: Goddamm.

—Ezra Pound, "Ancient Music"

13

Through the Ice Darkly

Foolish people—when I say "foolish people" in this contemptuous way, I mean people who entertain different opinions to mine. If there is one person I do despise more than another, it is the man who does not think exactly the same on all topics as I do.

—JEROME K. JEROME,
Idle Thoughts of an Idle Fellow

I wish I still drank enough to make ice fishing seem interesting. It would make Maine's long winters so much more entertaining and purposeful. Ice fishing I mean, not drinking. Not that drinking wouldn't make the winters more interesting, or at least less dreary—or so a lot of folks up this way seem to think, judging from the oceans of Allen's Coffee Brandy the corner store sells in the harsh stretch between Thanksgiving and mud season.

161

It's not that I don't drink at all. It's just that I don't drink very much: a glass of wine with dinner, maybe two if company's over and we're being convivial and jolly and they've brought along an extra bottle. And I'll drink a beer or two in summer when it's hot and I've been tilling under the spring crops and filling my lungs with dust and hen dressing, and I'll trudge up to the house and sit carefully downwind from my wife and her excessively sensitive nose, and blot my brow and wheeze all Dickensianly, "Whewww. Thustee wuhk out 'ere in the 'ot sun," and to keep me from tracking chickenshit all over the kitchen she'll go get me a Red Stripe, and I'll take a long pull from a frosty bottle and smile and smack my lips and go Awwwww, like a man in a beer commercial.

That's about it, though. Drinking I mean. Although I started early and practiced considerably, I just wasn't very good at it. I began drinking in high school as a way of appearing all tragic and consumed, hoping to forget a girl I'd loved and lost and, by way of compensation or revenge, hoping to arouse carnal interests in selected members of the hard-drinking Cool People clique. But I had no chance of penetrating that interspecies barrier no matter how tragic and consumed I got, for I played trumpet in the band and not quarterback on the football team, and I didn't own an overpowered car with loud mufflers and custom upholstery and didn't wear socks that matched my shirts. Worse, I wore bifocals, fished regularly, read unassigned books, got good grades, spoke in a circuitously peculiar fashion, and was so skinny that if I stood sideways and stuck out my tongue I looked like a zipper.

Cool Girls don't consider skinny, four-eyed, fish-chasing, trumpet-playing, book-reading, weird-talking brainiacs as possible mates, no matter how tragic and consumed. When you reel across the gym and drunkenly drip Poe and Byron all over their pom-poms and pleated skirts, they don't gaze into your soulful romantic eyes in a dizzy orbit of Valentine hearts and draw you tenderly to their letter-sweatered bosoms. They go Ewwwww and wish you dead, a desire their muscle-bound boyfriends tried to gratify numerous times as I drunkenly hurled Shakespearean barbs their way while they kicked the living shit out of me.

I didn't always drink but I did always talk in peculiar wandering circles, although my mother swore this didn't start until that summer I misread the Methodist Church Camp swimming pool and lost at King of the Mountain. At camp I had dived theatrically into a corner of the pool after reading its depth as eight feet instead of three: 8, 3—see how confusing? Especially when seen without my bifocals through the astigmatic glass of a cheap face mask. The next thing I remember was rising slowly to the surface as girls in frilly-bottomed bathing suits leapt screaming from a pinkening chlorinated froth. Picture the shark's-eye view of the beach in *Jaws,* only filmed through a camera with its lens smashed by a full bottle of Pepto-Bismol.

The doctors plucked shards of face mask from my face and tested my reflexes and swaddled my slightly cracked skull in a cotton turban, and in those pre-litigious times pronounced me fine and dandy. Then toward summer's end I was playing King of the Mountain with Harry Hartsook on the concrete retaining wall near his house. King of the Mountain, for those who grew up after Nintendo and obses-sive parenting supplanted unstructured outdoor play, is a game where one kid mounts the highest convenient elevation and pro-claims himself King, and his playmates attempt to abbreviate his reign by toppling him off. Just as I was exhorting my kingdom to make war upon the unnecessarily different and therefore unholy in-habitants of Rock Springs, Harry hooked an ankle and I hit the side-walk headfirst. My mother, hanging out laundry a hundred feet away, said it sounded like someone had tossed a watermelon off the back of a truck, and when she got there it looked like it, too.

After another session of head bandaging and reflex testing the doctor said I was fine, but my mother swore that after that summer I often acted as though I were "not right bright." Being not right bright would seem more advantage than disadvantage for someone hoping to mingle with the Cool People and know cheerleaders biblically, but apparently my version of not right bright never quite reached the socially acceptable level of testosteronal stupidity despite earnest efforts to drink my way there.

I am ashamed to confess an uncharitable satisfaction knowing that the most regal of those school-daze social queens—not the one who first broke my heart and lived ever after on a virginal pedestal but the one who later wriggled lasciviously through my nightly dreams and daily spurned my advances—now spends her days decoupaging Elvis ashtrays, dusting her husband's demolition-derby trophies, and dreaming of cashing in enough bottle deposits for a wild weekend at Dollywood with an inexpertly tattooed checkout clerk from the Piggly-Wiggly. Even as I type this I'm suppressing a smile and feeling horrible for doing it. Smiling I mean, not suppressing it. For as the passage in First Corinthians that donated this chapter's title inconveniently reminds me, I am no longer a child and must put away childish things. It also reminds me to be charitable above all else. And I'm trying. Honest. It's just that charity doesn't come easy when the mighty lie humbled. And there is nothing more entertainingly humble than formerly Cool People with a combined age of a century and a combined weight of a quarter ton trying to squeeze through the door of their house trailer with a case of beer under each arm.

But I vent. And gloat. And wander from the topic.

So after a few more years of reeling around like an anesthetized idiot with a tenuous toehold in two contradictory worlds and watching my grades go from As to Ds and worse, I joined the navy, and with my new government-issue muscles took up the sport of barroom brawling. This was always in the nature of a mission: About halfway through a night of recreational drinking a toothy smirking ectomorph would catch my eye and I would begin to torment him, commenting on his clothes, his girlfriend, his dim wits. And eventually he would take a swing at me, and I would duck and smile and take him apart. And the next morning I would feel all horrible and ridden with guilt, and would swear never to do this again and to always treat people as charitably as I wished to be treated myself. Then next weekend I'd get drunk and do it again.

Finally I ended my career as a tragic and consumed and increasingly belligerent drunk at a navy Christmas party, where I downed a fifth of Jack Daniel's, passed out with my head in the fireplace, and commenced to oxidize. After hasty fire-fighting efforts some holiday well-wishers lugged me downstairs and set me on the stoop to sober up, and when I awoke I was lying flat on my back and everything had gone white and cold. I thought I was dead again and on ice awaiting further instructions, but instead I had wandered off to a supermarket parking lot some two miles away and it had snowed. When I sat up slowly from beneath my white blanket, a smoke-blackened revenant creaking forth from his icy tomb, the woman just getting out of the car that had almost run me over screamed like Jamie Lee Curtis in *Halloween* and so did I, and when I awoke again I was lying under the bathroom sinks on the third floor of a navy barracks that looked like mine, but wasn't. And this is when I decided I had lost my taste for drinking, having already lost my taste for Cool People. And this is at least partly why when I moved to Maine and set about going native I couldn't develop a taste for ice fishing.

Of course while snow and ice are always part of the deal with ice fishing, drinking doesn't have to be. Up here it's a wholesome family sport and widely enjoyed. Ice fishing I mean. It's just that drinking seems the only way an angler not bred to it can numb the internal tedium meter and ignore ice fishing's inherent contradictions. And I am definitely not bred to it. Ice fishing I mean. Or drinking either, apparently.

The first time I saw frozen water that didn't come out of an ice cube tray was after I graduated from the navy and headed north in January of 1969. Near Harrisburg I crossed the Susquehanna River and noticed that it didn't look quite like any river I'd ever seen, so I pulled to the roadside and floundered down the embankment through half a foot of snow, and I knocked on the river with a stick and it rang like a door chime, and I said out loud, "Hail, 'at damn river's *froze*."

Since then I've lived continuously in the North—three years in Boston, thirty years in Maine—and over that time have seen a lot of frozen water but still can't warm to ice fishing.

I made my first ice-fishing trip nearly thirty years ago and in good company—a group of Maine-edition good ole boys twenty-five years my senior who had been ice fishing together proportionally as long as I had been fly fishing, which is to say all their lives. We walked out on the ice, triangulated a good fishing spot off the landmarks their fathers and grandfathers had shown them when they were small boys, then with a spud—a wicked huge tool that looks like Paul Bunyan's cold chisel—we chopped holes in the ice about a foot in diameter in a loose convivial circle.

When we got our holes cut and had spooned out the ice chips with big perforated ladles, we took our rigs from our pack baskets, unwound some monofilament from dinky little reels, stuck our hooks through the backs of shiners fished from bait buckets, then let out line to the bottom. Over the holes we set our rigs—called tip-ups, because when you get a bite that's what they do: tip up and set the hook and wave a little celebratory flag—then we sat there on our bait buckets in the cold wind with our feet on the ice, passing a bottle back and forth and talking of good times past and those yet to come and waiting for a flag to salute. When one did we'd reel in our fish, which with the water barely above freezing came up with little more fight than the shiners had made going down, and we skinned them out on the ice where they began to freeze solid, beginning with their eyeballs. If it was a legal-length trout or salmon it went home to fill the freezer, and if a short we worked the hook free and slid it back down the hole to swim in feeble aimless circles before fluttering limply to the bottom.

We sat there on the ice for hours, sliding back shorts and icing the occasional keeper, talking of our lives growing up in pursuit of fish and game and our love of the outdoors and of wild things in general, all the while passing a bottle back and forth. After a couple of pulls I waived my drinking rights, partly because I worried that killing all these short fish would make me maudlin and then perhaps belligerent, partly because I was feeling pretty squirrelly what with my previous experience mixing ice and snow and alcohol, and partly because the quaff du jour, a Maine brand of wine labeled Old Duke, tasted like Karo syrup mixed with Drygas and Raid.

By the next winter I had fallen in with a different crowd, men more my own age who fly fished pretty hard throughout the spring and summer and ice fished pretty hard throughout the winter, sitting over holes in the ice passing a bottle around and talking as their fathers did of days gone by and days yet to come, of fish and deer and moose and women we loved or would like to love and jobs we hated but could see no way out of having. We didn't set tip-ups but instead used miniature spinning rods, jigging little metal lures up and down, up and down, and taking nice trout and salmon and releasing many shorts—more carefully this time, more easily, for the fish didn't automatically swallow the jigs as they did bait but took the jigs in the lip as they would a fly, and we could twist them free with the fish safely in the water.

But with each trout and each salmon that came meekly to the surface, pale monochrome shadows of their fleet and flashing summertime selves, I thought how much more enjoyable to have caught them from a cool forest run or a great roiling river, with the fish running and leaping and incandescing in the sun, and how dull to have dragged them unceremoniously through a hole chopped in the ice while passing around a bottle and talking of unrequited love, or perhaps more accurately, unrequited lust.

And then I got married again and found more emotionally and physically rewarding ways to spend cold winter days than staring into the cold and rhythmically moving my hand up and down. And a few years later we reproduced, and our son grew up with a fisherman for a father but took no interest in fishing—not the lovely laughing brooks that everywhere thread the New England woods, nor the quiet dappled ponds where brook trout rise in the sunset, nor the remote loon-haunted lakes where landlocked salmon cruise endlessly, never mind shivering on the ice in testicle-shrinking cold while staring down a hole waiting for a chilled trout's flaccid bite.

I date Ethan's dislike of fish and fishing from when he was a baby and we sometimes had trouble finding quality child care after Linda resumed teaching in the fall, and I would stuff him into a Snugli baby carrier, a little corduroy baby snood that straps onto your chest and leaves your hands free for other things, and take him out lobstering for the day. For hours the pothauler would hurl a continuous stream of salt water and seaweed at the back of his little Sesame Street cap, and he would breathe an unpleasant stew of salted herring cuttings, diesel fumes, and hardworking smelly daddy while the exhaust roared like a constipated lion as I gunned the engine from trap to trap, the rain cap tap-tap-tapping at idle while diving gulls screamed for leftover bait like extras in *The Birds*.

I had thought the boat's rocking would lull him to sleep and he would enjoy being in the out-of-doors and bonding with Deare Olde Dadde. I mean *I* enjoyed it; why shouldn't he? But he didn't. Now, not only won't he go fishing, he won't even stay in the house when fish is cooking. Perhaps my mother was right after all. About my sometimes acting not right bright I mean.

So without the excuse of inculcating my son with the fishing lore he didn't want or infusing my brain with the alcohol it had proved incapable of handling, I drifted away from ice fishing. And over the years ice fishing drifted away from me, becoming more a mechanized assault on a resource than a friendly trip into the woods for a drink or two and some dirty jokes and a salmon for supper. Instead of triangulating hot spots off landmarks passed down from father to son, the new ice fishers tracked down schools of fish using through-the-ice sonar. Instead of chopping a few holes through the ice with spuds, the new ice fishers drilled long strings of holes in seconds with chain-saw engined ice augers and moved their tip-ups from hole to hole, bracketing schools of fish like artillery probing a target. Instead of the quiet empty peace of the boreal winter, the ponds and lakes filled with the nasty sulfurous snarl of ice augers and whizzing snowmobiles.

Families still ice fished together and folks still loved the sport passionately, but the majority who practiced good sportsmanship and respected the wild seemed increasingly overshadowed by the minority who did not. Game wardens staking out remote lakes found wholesale violations of bag limits and saw short fish being released by methods best described as brutal even by bait-fishing standards. Not that ice fishing has the market cornered on poor sportsmanship; just watch a professional football game or a basketball game. Better yet, go to a Little League game and watch the parents. Or check out the proliferation of "game farms," where "sportsmen" blast away at exotic animals confined in close paddocks. Blind self-interest and winning at all costs seem the early favorites for defining the twenty-first century. Sometimes I wish I still drank enough so I wouldn't notice.

And over the years fly fishing changed, too, becoming less the province of Thoreauvian tree huggers, eggheaded social misfits, and philosophical head twiddlers who enjoyed a chess match with a master of survival and stealth out there in the clean wild woods and more a trendy sport practiced at name-brand venues by Cool People.

I ran into one such ascendant individual a few years back on a well-fished nearby pond, and as we chatted briefly I found out he had moved to southern Maine from Massachusetts about five years previously and had taken to fly fishing with the novitiate's burning fervor, and that he had found the fishing poor this spring and that he blamed ice fishermen for coming in over the winter and cleaning out all the fish, and that the best thing the state could do would be to ban ice fishing so there would be more fish for true sportsmen such as him and, nodding toward my fly rod, me.

And as he spoke I nodded and shrugged and made noncommittal little throat sounds and tried to seem attentive, but I didn't really hear him talking about how we fly fishermen had the economic clout to force ice fishermen off the ice but heard instead the Cool People back in high school talking about how so-and-so was just *too* gross and smelled of the *pigs* his father kept and they were just so *poor,* and how they couldn't *believe* whosi-whatsis had the nuts to try out for Beta Club no matter *what* kind of grades he got because he was just so *lame* and his mother took in *washing,* and how what's-his-face hadn't even *read* that book but had nonetheless gotten a *C* on his book report because he scored a touchdown every time he *touched* a football and what teacher would *dare* flunk him with the *big game* coming, and . . .

And I thought back to my second summer in Maine when I was fishing a little brook with my dad and he had asked how my first Maine winter had gone, and I told him I'd spent most of it sawing four times more firewood than I thought I'd need and shoveling ten times more snow than I'd ever seen, and that I had discovered when you peed in the outhouse at thirty-five below zero it sounded like glass breaking and if you sat down you would literally freeze to the seat, but that I did get out snowshoeing a fair amount and loved rambling aimlessly through the glittering silent cathedral of the winter woods, and that I had gone ice fishing half a dozen times with some local guys and had tried to like it but had not succeeded.

He asked what ice fishing was like, and I thought for a while and said it was like sitting in the supermarket freezer trying to hook a package of Mrs. Paul's Fish Sticks, only colder and not as compelling. And that the number of short fish we had inadvertently killed had probably outnumbered the legal fish we purposefully killed by ten to one, and that this seemed like a peculiar thing to do for folks who professed to love the outdoors and all. And he asked why anyone would want to do it. Ice fish, he meant. And I thought for a while and finally said it was a pretty damn good excuse to sit outside drinking and telling rancid jokes and pretending to rustle up supper, and that there wasn't a helluva lot else for folks to do up here in winter, and the folks who did it genuinely seemed to enjoy it. And then I said, Well, you know, they're not like us. And by that I meant fly fishermen.

And then the present day snapped back into focus, and I remembered I was nodding and smiling absently as another accomplished and fervent fly fisherman said, "You know, they're not like us." And by that he meant ice fishermen.

And I said that in many ways they *were* like us, in that privately exploiting a public resource provides a plausible reason to linger outside under the wide sky with the wind at our backs and the smell of balsam fir in our noses, and that although some of *them* were demonstrably deficient in sportsmanship it seemed an increasing number of *us* were getting that way, too, and that Maine and other northern states had tens of thousands of square miles of lakes and ponds and that the best of them were already being converted to fly fishing only, and didn't it seem charitable and fair to leave the rest of the water for them to fish, considering as how there were so many more of them than there were of us, and that they enjoyed sitting out on the ice jigging for trout and gulping cheap wine just as much as we enjoyed matching hatches and sipping single-malt Scotch?

And as he turned red and notched up the them-and-us argument I said, Well of course I could be wrong, and maybe fly fishers should have first pick of all the best water because we truly respect it, and what did I know anyway? Then we shook hands and went our separate ways, for as I mentioned earlier I no longer drink enough to make lots of things seem interesting, including goading people into meaningless fights I knew I could win, for I had learned over the years they were invariably part of a larger battle I knew I would always lose.

14

Those Who Say Woo

> *Serious sport has nothing to do with fair play. It is bound up with hatred, jealousy, boastfulness, disregard of all rules and sadistic pleasure in witnessing violence: in other words it is war minus the shooting.*
>
> —GEORGE ORWELL,
> "The Sporting Spirit"

With fishing season past and football season in full swing, I feel faint twinges of those deep-rooted urges that have long brought men together. I feel them, but I rarely act on them, for even though I am biologically compelled to sit before the TV watching the clean-cut amateur athletes of the University of Tennessee Volunteers stomp big greasy mudholes in the hired hooligans of the Godless Florida Gators and other unsavory life-forms, I do so alone.

I attribute this couch-potato solitaire to three factors, the first being that I live in Maine, where other men biologically compelled to share the University of Tennessee football team's triumphs and disappointments are few and far between; the second being that for personal biological reasons I limit my consumption of alcohol, which is the mother's milk of these gatherings and the prime motivator behind every group of men who ever appeared on national television with their naked bellies sequentially lettered GO VOLS BEAT BAMA. The third reason is my congenital inability to say Woo.

And when men come together to commit or witness acts of public sportsmanship, there is always much saying of Woo: When a touchdown punches in, or a home run clears the left-field fence, or a three-pointer swishes the net, or a massé shot sinks the one-ball and the cue draws back and drops the nine, all witnessing males, and increasing numbers of females, must Woo loudly and often and slap high-fives, handshakes being passé among true sayers of Woo.

These raucous communal celebrations of tribal competition, with their vestigial whiffs of pogroms and witch burnings, have taken over fly fishing, too, and this sends a shudder down my stiff spine. Not so much because others enjoy doing it—who am I to prescribe the behavior of others?—but because I, a minor member of the fish media, am expected to take part and am viewed suspiciously when I don't.

This inability to join in any reindeer games is why you're unlikely ever to see my wizened face on a TV fishing show, and why you'll rarely see me fishing with a guide unless mandated by law or convention.

I have nothing against TV. I like TV. I grew up with TV. I watch way more TV than I ought, especially in winter when it's dark and gloomy and fishing season's over and there's a good movie on with Gene Tierney looking quizzical or Veronica Lake bemused. But because I watch TV regularly I know what telegenic is, and telegenic I ain't.

And I've nothing against guides, either. Some of my best friends are guides. My brother is a guide. But most guides, particularly young guides or some western guides or most Florida Keys guides, bring to what one fly-fishing magazine calls the Quiet Sport an unwelcome dose of competition; worse, they are—by reasons of nature and nurture and, it must be said, expectant profitability—unable to do what I wish all guides would do when I'm fishing with them, which is hunt up some shade and take a nap while I figure out for myself how to catch a fish. To me the pleasure is more in the puzzle than in the catching. If I want help I won't be shy about asking for it. If I catch a fish and my guide or otherwise companion simply cannot throttle tribal urges, a simple handshake will do, perhaps a Nicely Done if whatever I happened to do actually was. I do not wish, merely because I have caught a fish, to jump up and down slapping vertical palms and hooting Woo like an amphetamined Mousketeer.

I was not raised in a demonstrative family. When one of us caught a fish and someone was in earshot we'd say Got One. If a big fish, we'd say Looks Like a Nice-un. And if a great thumping leviathan, we'd dole out a mildly italicized adjective and say Looks Like a *Rill* Nice-un.

Neither were we competitive. If one of us caught more fish than the other, we were happy he did and said so. If the one who caught more fish did so by imaginatively tweaking customary techniques, he'd happily share his secrets. If one of us caught few or no fish, he was not teased unmercifully and made to feel like an evolutionary aberration. We were merely enjoying the pleasant puzzle of catching fish with flies in our own small fashion, not competing for bragging rights with rival tribes.

Humans seem incapable of doing anything without turning it into a competition—enlisting supporters, demonizing opponents, ostracizing detractors. From the executive suite to the presidential campaign, billfish tournaments to one-fly competitions, we all strive constantly to best the other, a nonstop pissing contest graded on length, volume, and degree of artistic flourishes.

For this I blame beer. Not alcohol, mind you: beer.

Six thousand years ago the Sumerians brought humanity the intertwined twin gifts of organized civilization and a fermented beverage brewed from the cultivated grains that made civilization possible. Centuries later, after constant warfare among the Sumerian city-states over, I hypothesize, the formula for what in years to come would be known as Sam Adams, the Babylonians became Top Nation and their king, Hammurabi, enacted a set of laws that, among other things, codified the rationing of beer—common worker ants got two liters a day, while the priesthood and other deserving glitterati got five. The wise Hammurabi even provided strict guidelines for how purveyors of bad beer might be killed: drowning.

The fierce Gauls battled the wine-drinking Romans while hopped up on beer. Later, both got decisively stomped by the Germanic tribes, who had not only better beer but also the promise of, should they die in battle contesting their foes, winning eternal life in a heaven where bosomy blondes served forth beer from bottomless barrels in an endless celestial frat party. If you watch the commercials that accompany all televised sporting events, you'll note this is still our collective idea of heaven, with scantily clad bimbettes bearing bounteous beer to Victorious Men as their envious admirers leap about shouting Woo.

I have not, as befits an inquiring mind, based my theory on the interrelationship among beer, male bonding, and cutthroat competition entirely on the writings of dusty historians. I have scientific proof.

It was a typical Penobscot expedition with the usual suspects—Will, Tom, Marcel, and Shawn being the core group, with weekend appearances by Vic, Ralph, and Terry. By typical I mean it was raining like a cow pissing on a flat rock, and we were taking an extended midday break beneath the tarp and quietly making fun of the white-water rafters floating by. The core group has been making this trip since college days and thus a kind of collegiate flavor permeates camp, meaning there's more than a bit of recreational drinking and much unhygienic slovenliness. Empty cans and bottles tend to collect on the table among a litter of fly-tying vises and potato chip bags; middle-aged men with smoldering cigars and eyeballs carved out of bacon slouch around in gaping disarray; the surrounding forest looks as though a flock of Easter chicks had been slaughtered with tennis rackets, the multicolored marabou fallout from Will's enormous smelt streamers tied slowly and inattentively in the wind.

Given the relentless downpour that had driven away less dedicated or perhaps more energetic campers, there was little else to see in the riverside campground but us, and the hormonally chuffed white-water rafters always looked our way as they drifted by, sometimes seeming not to see us, sometimes looking away in disgust, sometimes pumping clinched fists—the long-distance version of a high-five—and shouting Woo.

Over time this began to prey on my mind, which tends toward unnecessary scientific investigations and wasn't, unlike those of my campmates, especially befuddled by alcohol, recreational drinking being for me more a spectator than a participant sport. And because my campmates were by then in varying degrees of befuddlement and thus easily led, I drafted them for an experiment.

We cleared the table of liquor bottles and beer cans—no small accomplishment I can tell you—and placed in drinking positions an assortment of Cokes, Pepsis, Mountain Dews, and other puritanically appropriate beverages consisting of equal parts sugar and carbonated water. Two rafts drifted by, and although the occupants all looked our way we were to them merely inanimate background, like trees, a tent, or a Dumpster. As they cleared the lip of the pool and entered the first small haystacks and souse holes, they paddled indifferently, as though the driving rain had sapped their spirits of tribal teamwork and they wanted only to see their lackluster lives end as painlessly and as soon as possible.

Then we cleared away the soft drinks and crowded on a dozen or so liquor bottles in varying degrees of emptiness, and we poured transparent plastic cups half full of amber beverages and waited. Two more rafts drifted by, and the occupants uniformly viewed us with scorn and loathing, as though we were cockroaches toes-up in their crème brûlée or derelicts facedown in our own vomit. Aflame with indignation, they entered the rapids digging at the water in angry arrhythmic jabs, as though to punish it for sins against society.

Then we cleared away the liquor bottles and covered the table with beer cans, and the next two raftloads that came by looked our way, and their faces lit up and their arms pumped up and down, and from across the river came a chorus of *Wooooo, Woooooo,* punctuated by the occasional *Yesssssss* and *Awriiiiiight,* and they hit the white water pulling together like oarsmen at the Henley Regatta and exhibiting that modern-day bonding-in-the-wilderness bravado that makes me want to flush Robert Bly's head down an iron john.

We went through this sequence a dozen or more times during the next several hours of relentless rain and experimentation and saw no deviation in rafter reactions. The mere sight of beer welded a raft full of unrelated humans into a team of latter-day Vikings who bonded with those happy slouching layabouts on the bank and then felt the need to show them a thing or two about how Real by God He-Men laugh at recreational drowning for the greater glory of Raft Number 227. You could almost hear the television cameras whirring as a team of beer-bearing babes dropped from the sky.

∾   ∾   ∾   ∾   ∾   ∾

I'm sure it's only a matter of time before fly-fishing TV moves past its current fireplace-video placidity into Competition as Televised Extravaganza, where hushed crowds watch in suspense as Celebrity Fly Fisher flexes his mighty rod and drops a tiny dun on the upstream edge of a rise ring, and when the trout takes and he sets the hook, his many fans will leap about and shout Woo and slap their palms together, and bulbous male bellies will be bared to reveal painted letters spelling SAGE and ORVIS and SPARKLE DUNS RULE.

And then the camera will tighten in on an announcer with a beer-company crest embroidered on his Ex Officio shirt, and in hushed tones he'll explain the significance of what we've just seen and tell us how thrilled we all are to have seen it, and then, his face creased with smiles and his mellifluous voice drizzling he-man hormones, he'll say And Now It's Miller Time.

And it is for me, too, or at least Guinness time, for Tennessee and Arkansas are playing in a few minutes, and all this talk about beer has worked up a powerful thirst. Besides, I'll need to be properly adjusted, just in case the clean-cut heroic University of Tennessee Volunteers need my moral support in their victory over the Razorback rabble, a quiet tribal hoot from an insignificant corner of the State of Maine, where the fishing season is closed and there's little else to do but sit in the dark alone and whisper, *Woo.*

15

Little Big Business

I wish I could remember which of history's great quoticians wrote, "Commerce cheapens us all." I'd like to go and sit beside her grave, and light candles, and gaze wistfully at her tombstone, and contemplate the loss of such concise enveloping wisdom as tears well slowly from my eyes and drop one by one to nourish sweet violets twining below.

What launched this weepy interlude is the loom of Christmas season, that curious blend of ancient pagan celebrations of rebirth co-opted by fourth-century Christians for a commemorative membership drive and later by twentieth-century merchants to boost year-end cash flow. As another of history's great quoticians more or less said about the American economy, If Christmas had not existed it would have been necessary to invent it.

If you think about it, the commercial side of Christmas has a lot in common with fly fishing. The fun lies in the anticipation, the poring through of books and catalogs, the acquisition of knowledge and matériel and sly intelligence, the selection of offerings, the approach, the packaging, the presentation—all those things that go into giving or getting a gift or catching a fish on a fly. And once the elaborate wrappings are off and you and/or yours have thrilled and/or blanched at getting and/or giving a first-edition of Haig-Brown or a shiny necktie desecrated with Royal Coachmans or a box of naughty chocolates or a complete illustrated history of something someone once mentioned as being vaguely interesting, you're left with a small cavity that yearns to be filled with More.

We acquire this acquisitive hunger when we're young and Mommy and Daddy tell us that if we're very good, Father Christmas will bring us a Lionel train or a Gilbert chemistry set or G.I. Joe or Barbie and Ken or a Megaman Fortress of Gloom and Disappointment Adventure Playset or whatever it is Santa's little helpers, by which I mean Christmas catalogs and the relentless psychological warfare campaign that used to begin at Thanksgiving and now commences around Labor Day, have convinced us we cannot live without.

When we become nominal adults we acquire new and expensive and often very specialized longings. We pore endlessly through catalogs and advertisements and Web pages tailored to help us gratify them, everything from sports cars to wine to audio equipment to cat memorabilia to, of course, fly rods and reels and lines and leaders and on and on and on.

We get hooked when we watch others fly fishing and see how beautiful and peaceful it looks, and when we catch our first fish on a fly we want another and another, and when we catch our first big fish we want another even bigger, and we'll spend whatever time and money we can spare and sometimes time and money we can't spare on the books and fly rods and waders and boats and chaperoned trips into the back of beyond that we hope will lead us to More. We are important economic stimuli, us fly fisherfolk hungering after More, all two to eleven million of us, depending on which breathless industry booster's research you believe, digging deeply into our wallets in the intertwined names of sport and commerce.

Of late I'm feeling a bit too intertwined with commerce. Like most members of my self-deluded generation, I fancy myself a sophisticated consumer immune to marketing machinations, but my credit-card statements say otherwise, and so do endless shelves and drawers and forgotten boxes groaning with unnecessary necessities I had once convinced myself I could not live without.

I honestly don't know how many fly rods I own. I don't really think I want to. I do know I have all but four of the fly rods I've managed to acquire over four decades of relentless acquisition. One of the missing, a ratty old Montague Mount Tom with rickety guides and an over-the-rainbow set, went to the dump when I bought a shiny white Shakespeare Wonderod along around 1959. The other three—a good Heddon, a great Edwards, and a so-so Orvis of redundant lengths and line weights—got traded to Bob Gorman for one of his cracking little split-cane small-stream specials. And as for reels and waders and fly boxes and vises and feathers and fur and lines and leaders and books and more books and on and on? Lord knows how much there is. Tons, probably.

I keep thinking I ought to donate some of it to Trout Unlimited or FFF or a new fly fisher long on enthusiasm and short on cash, or run an ad in one of the fly-fishing magazines and sell most of it off, or hold a yard sale of my own, or even open a tackle shop. But then I'll screw the cap off a rod tube I haven't picked up in years, and I'll wrap my hand around the grip all brown with sweat and bug dope and dusted with pearlescent fish scales, its aft end all chewed up with the flies I know I shouldn't stick in the corks of good rods but can't stop doing, and I'll remember fishing this rod on the Madison or the Miramichi or the Tellico or the Penobscot or under the Chesapeake Bay Bridge, and I'll remember a nice brown or a salmon or a rainbow or a smallmouth or a striper that was just a hair dumber than I was that day, and I'll remember the people I was with and the music the river played and how the birds sang and how the water looked in the sun or the rain and what we had for dinner that night in the cabin or around the fire or in the corner of a little Eastern Shore crab shack or the parking lot of the Tellico Beach Drive-In, and I'll slide it back into the tube, screw down the cap, and lean it back in the corner with the rest of the rods I'm no more able to get rid of than the cheesy plastic second-place trophy from the local five-and-dime's model-car-building contest that was the high point of my ninth year, or the wedding pictures from a short-lived marriage that became the low point of my twenty-first year, or the wheezy clanking refrigerator with the marks on its door tracking our son's year-to-year progress from toddler to, if it had been a foot taller, a man.

And then I'll think, Well, at least my wants are simple and I've got everything I need. And then I'll walk to town and get the mail and, at this most wonderful time of the year, come back laden with catalogs from Orvis and Kaufmann's and Madison River Fishing Company, and I'll see cool new stuff I think I need but probably don't, and out will come the phone and credit card and then a few days later Vinnie will come bouncing up the drive in his UPS truck and I'll have More.

The quest for More is a problem for most fly fishers, but for fish writers it's also an occupational hazard. Every year I go to the fly-fishing industry trade show and sift through windrows of new equipment, looking for something significant or superlative or simply cool that folks who read my little fish column might want to know about. And every year I'll find a few things I really like, and I'll borrow review samples from the manufacturers and I'll go play with them, and if after a few months of field trials the reality lives up to the hype and my first heated impressions, I'll write something nice in the one issue each year where I talk about the toys instead of what gets done with them, and then instead of packing up the newly reviewed toys and sending them back to the companies as I ought, I'll call their media contacts and give them my credit-card number, and I'll own still more things I don't really need but briefly believed I could not live without.

More. With fly fishing there's always More. The only thing I see less of in fly fishing is the companies that make the More.

I like small family restaurants with hand-lettered menus, imaginative daily specials, a stainless-steel milk cooler papered over with crayon drawings and report cards, old-line staff and old-line customers bantering away while hand-patted hamburgers sizzle on the grill. I like dusty hardware stores with oiled wooden floors, tin bins full of galvanized nails, a boxful of lamp wicks beside a ka-chinging old cash register, and a shuffling old man in a saggy cardigan who knows precisely what weird widget you want from your incomplete description. I love hole-in-the-wall ship chandleries reeking of pine tar and salt and verdigris and pipe smoke where grizzled men wearing rolled-down hip boots lean back on rope bales and shamelessly embellish hair-raisers about their own perfect storms. I love lobsters and shrimp and crabs and haddock sold from the backs of rusty pickup trucks by the cantankerous old farts who caught them, and little roadside farm stands where entrepreneurial adolescents stand proudly behind stacks of old-fashioned sweet corn, soft red tomatoes, and delicate ripe raspberries they'd picked only an hour before.

I dislike worldwide restaurant chains with menus devised by focus groups and spreadsheets, and interiors as sterile and unsettling as a proctologist's exam glove. I don't care for mega home centers that have everything except what you need and no one there who can answer a question no matter how simple it is. I hate acres-wide boating centers that smell of fiberglass and finance charges and the aftershaves of briskly blazered Tads and Todds wearing new Top-Siders and captain's caps with a dozen eggs freshly scrambled on the brim. I loathe "fresh" seafood flown in from wherever in the world the corporate sea-vacuums found something still alive and at least nominally legal. I despise sprawling supermarkets filled with fake food grown in the fertile fields of fourth-quarter profits.

But because I am a modern American, I am forever finding myself in all those places I don't like for the simple reason that it's getting harder and harder to find the kinds of places I do. Local restaurants wither away as publicly traded fast-fooderies arrive in a haze of golly-gee advertising. Mom-and-pop motels go belly-up when brand-name multinationals come to the neighborhood. Small family-run stores go out of business left and right as big-box retailers move to town and briefly lower prices.

Big companies swallow little companies, and still bigger companies then swallow them. Our local cable TV company has been bought four times in the past ten years; our phone company, our bank, our Internet service provider, the newspaper, our local supermarket, and the book publisher I used to work for have all been bought three times. Not once in all these corporate swallowings has anything gotten better, or cheaper, or in any way more satisfying for the customer; usually everything gets worse except the executive compensation packages of the company that did the swallowing. The one thing that always changes is who gets your money, and how much of it they get.

And this is true in the big little business of fly fishing, too.

It seems hardly a month passes without some favorite old name in fly fishing getting gobbled up. Press releases assure us that, Oh Yes, so-and-so the Behemoth Retailer and so-and-so the Cutting-Edge Innovator have Joined Forces, and never fear, because the Much Revered innovative brand names will go on Exactly As Before; it's just that to improve Efficiencies and provide greater Economies of Scale and Expand the Market we've found it best to Merge Our Assets, which is business-school-speak for We'll make more money if we have fewer competitors, especially if they're innovative and nimble but, alas for them and lucky for us, a little short on cash flow.

Unlike the recent rash of mega mergers among media giants and airlines that have dominated the news these past few years, most of those in the fly fishing business have been less acts of corporate predation than opportunistic bottom feeding on businesses run not by businessmen but by fly fishermen who only incidentally were in business.

Given the tiny and quasi-collegiate nature of the fly-fishing business, I know most of the people involved, sellers and buyers alike, and for the most part they're pretty nice people. Some are even friends and fishing buddies, about equally split between small-scale artisans and executives of mega companies. But businesspeople are businesspeople. They do what's best for business, which is relentlessly acquire More. More is what's best for business, even if that business is fly fishing, and even if more fishers buying more fishing equipment means less water for everyone to fish.

On a grand scale, there's little I can do about all this merger mania. When a multinational oil company nastier than most buys a couple of regional oil companies that at least try to play fair by the weak standards of their business, will I drive an hour to buy gas from a more palatable competitor? When the oversized airline that drove away the midsized airline from our nearby airport by pushing cut-rate seats cuts the number of those seats and ups its prices 50 percent, will I drive five hours to the urban airport where competition still keeps fares low? In both cases, probably not.

But when small innovative fly-fishing businesses that made things I always liked get swallowed up by large fly-fishing businesses whose primary market advantages are a wide product line, deep pockets, a huge corporate parent, and a talent for shifting manufacturing operations from high-cost domestic suppliers where folks like you and me earn a living wage and have enough time off to go fly fishing now and then to low-cost overseas operations where living wages and time off are as rare as ten-pound brook trout, what do I do then?

Professionally speaking, I have no options. As a member of the fish media, I have to say accurate things about new equipment whether or not I like the folks who make it, whether or not their business practices meet my narrow and probably unrealistic view of right and wrong. It's not easy, because there are folks I like and folks I dislike on both sides of the big-business/little-business divide. But a fly-fishing writer presuming to say one rod is good and another is not so good mustn't let issues of friendship or enmity get in the way, even if it pisses off people you genuinely like and delights people you don't.

But as a consumer . . . well, I'm free to vote my conscience with my pocketbook, no matter what the business.

If Linda and I wake up wanting hamburgers, and a TV ad blitz tells us McDonald's is trying to inconvenience Burger King by selling thirty-cent burgers this week only, you can figure on us being at the drive-up window by noon, filling a bag with loss-leader burgers and saying No Thanks to the immensely profitable french fries and Coke.

If we want a real burger and we're too shiftless to make it ourselves, we'll go down to the town wharf and visit Aunt Vi's Lunch Wagon, where Cher will make us beautiful handmade hamburgers and tell us how her daughter's doing at school.

If we want to see a movie and are too impatient to wait out a two-dollar video release, we'll go to the little family-owned Colonial in Belfast and shun the big-ticket stock-exchange-listed multiplex in Bangor.

If we want a steak or bananas or milk or eggs or a big puffy doughnut and a newspaper, we'll head for Tozier's Market down at the end of our street, where the prices are within spitting distance of the imperious chain-store supermarket down the road but the quality is light-years better and the owner is manning a broom and stocking the shelves and not smugly toting up profits in the executive suite of an immense European conglomerate.

If I need a fly line or a leader and don't have the time or inclination to go through the often complex process of buying directly from the manufacturer at a steep discount—a widespread industry benefit most writers and guides happily use, the high end manufacturers' viewpoint being that it would send the wrong message if clients or readers saw a guide or a writer actually catching fish with the low-end rods and reels our modest wages would incline us to buy—I'll search out a small fly shop where the owners and the salesclerks are one and the same.

I'd pay about the same for a line or leader at the little neighborhood fly shop or a mom-and-pop mail-order outfit as I would at a big glossy cataloger or e-tailer, except that I'd know half of every dollar goes directly to the owner, who has taught so many local boys and girls how to fish in his free classes and always knows what weather is coming, where the big ones are hiding, and what they're hitting. And if I need some flies and don't have time to tie them, I'll certainly buy them there, too. Maybe they'll cost twenty-five cents more than the flies in the pretty catalog pictures, and they might not be the latest hot patterns, but at least I'll know that, except for the tax man's slice, every penny of that $2.50 goes to the tier, and not to a mega retailer's profits and endless advertising, leaving only a few pennies for the Third World starvelings living seven to the sampan who actually tied it.

But because I'm a modern American, I can carry this marketplace purism only so far. If a behemoth company comes out with a rod or a reel or a line that sets a new benchmark for performance, I'll almost certainly convince myself I need to buy one, whether I approve of the company or not.

And if a behemoth company I view with suspicion buys a little innovator I've always liked, I'll still probably buy the stuff they sell under the good old name, unless the behemoth cheapens the stuff or changes it in ways that make it less than it was before. Then they're fair game, and I can go after them with journalistic guns blazing. And because I'm a modern American, I'll even be able to pretend my sniping isn't personal, because it's all just business.

16

The Vice of the Vise

To hear the winds burst with ferocious might
their prison gates and clash with martial sound—
this is the winter, such are its delights.

—ANTONIO VIVALDI, *The Four Seasons*

As it was in the beginning, so shall it be in the end: I'm slouched in an Adirondack chair in the office, tiny computer balanced across my lap, coffee steaming on the armrest as I piddle around writing inconsequential tales of fish and fishing. Only instead of a perfect springtime symphony playing in the background I have for my morning listening enjoyment the building howl of a northeast gale, the rising wind razzing the weather stripping like a medicated blues kazoo backed up by the percussive splats of wet snow against glass. And I'm doing less piddling around with words than a middle-aged man ought who needs to finish one book and start another, who owes articles to two magazines and belated Christmas cards to people who remembered me better than I did them. Mostly, though, I'm not doing any of the things I should be doing. Instead, I'm letting the computer screen go dark and the belated Christmas cards sit empty of sentiments while I idly lash feathers and fur to fishhooks, investing inanimate objects with the breath of life, or hoping to.

As fly tiers go, I'm not much. My eyes are weak and at close range increasingly move out of synch with my stiffening fingers. But I've always lacked the Zen patience and micromechanical ability of a real fly tier, so the new physical failings aren't so much roadblocks as simply additional speed bumps on what has always been a slow and winding road.

I can tie flies well enough to meet my own needs, meaning they're good enough to fool enough fish to keep me happily fishing, but they're not those tiny works of art shown off so proudly to other anglers, as flies tend to be when other anglers meet. When I'm maneuvered into showing off a fly, I usually haul out one my brother tied. I never claim I tied it, of course, but I don't volunteer the information that I didn't tie it, either. When directly questioned, I will of course say my brother tied it, and that he's been tying since the age of nine and has flies in the American Museum of Fly Fishing and all that kind of stuff, and from his accomplishments I'll gain a small measure of pride. And then as an act of contrition I'll show off a fly or two I tied—a nondescript little beadhead caddis larva, or a raggedy Parachute Hare's Ear, or a muddled Muddler—and I'll laugh and say how lucky I am that most trout aren't as discriminating as the literature makes them out to be.

For me, tying flies is less a path to accomplishment than a backdoor escape, a convenient way to blot up crumbs of useful time that might otherwise be turned to profitable use, to let the words I'm supposed to be writing stew a bit longer before I have to write them, to duck out on the tedious preparations for the wrath-of-God blizzard the wild-eyed TV weatherman raves is on its way and whole crowds of other pressing adulthood responsibilities. The vises—an old Thompson clamped to the desk too temptingly close to the keyboard and a new rotary perched on the arm of this Adirondack chair—are always patiently waiting to lead me astray with their hungry open jaws, and I always have hooks and feathers and furs and bits of shiny tinsel and sparkly synthetics ready to feed them. It is, if you will, a small vice of the vise—the harmless twiddling away of immediate responsibilities in hopes of gaining some distant future contentment.

So much of fly fishing is about twiddling away responsibilities—taking to the river, trending into the wild, packing up all those cares and woes, here I go, singing low, like Huck and Jim on the raft. That's fly fishing's primary charm, or at least it is to me: its sheer time-wasting silliness, the endless hours spent digesting vast amounts of arcane knowledge of no practical benefit beyond fooling a fish you then let go. If fly fishing were useful I'd probably find some other way to, as another song goes, fritter and waste the hours in an offhand way.

I have spent a lifetime trying to become a better fly fisher, but as the years fly by and I look back with a middle-aged man's regret at things I wish I'd done and things I wish I hadn't, I find I want to be a better person more than I want to be a better fly fisherman. Curiously, I think striving to become the latter has nudged me at least a little way toward becoming the former. I know that sounds all smarmy and pretentious and holier-than-thou—I shook out a Nyquil shudder as I wrote those words—but I know it to be true.

Fly fishers notice the environment in ways nonfishers don't—the direction and velocity of the wind, the position of the sun and the phase of the moon, what bugs are in the bushes or in the water, how the water sweeps and flows and angles around unseen structure, providing restful places for fish to linger and await the hydraulic delivery of dinner. If we don't notice all this stuff and understand what it means, we simply won't catch fish.

When fly fishing I behave better toward people than I might otherwise—giving a healthy buffer of privacy to someone already fishing a pool, yielding right-of-way on the stream when it's proper, unobtrusively educating someone who might happen to know less than I do about some obscure and absent detail standing between fisher and fish. If I don't do these things, when it comes time for someone to leave me in peace to fish the pool I'm in, or to yield right-of-way as I fish upstream and him down, or to show me how to do something I don't know how to do without making me feel like an idiot for not knowing it, it's likely they won't do any of those things. It's that optimistic Golden Rule thing in its original do-unto-others-as-you-would-have-them-do-unto-you version, before we began evolving from kind and generous brothers and sisters of the angle sharing quiet days on the stream into Ambrose Bierce's definition of a pessimist, which is someone who thinks everyone is as nasty as himself and hates them for it.

Fly fishing forces me to think the best of my fellow fishers. Even if a measurable percentage are pompous horse's asses and insufferable strutting gasbags, the vast majority are pleasant folk who fly fish for the same reasons I do, which is to pursue through beautiful surroundings something not easily obtained while gaining nothing beyond self-pleasure and a small measure of spiritual renewal.

Fly fishing forces me to slow down and if not actually smell the roses at least take the time to untangle my line from them, and from the gorse and the heather and the aspen and the birch and all the other bankside flora my inattentive backcasts are wont to explore. If my head weren't stuck up a tree, trying to retrieve my fly and unweave my leader, would I really notice the intricate patterns in hemlock bark, or the way spruce cones form like tiny green buds? If my wandering flies didn't get caught beneath all those river-bottom rocks, would I notice what those rocks were made of? Would I care if they were limestone or granite, or bother to study the geology of a river so that I might better understand its insect life and therefore catch more of its trout?

Before I go off fishing, I'm a middle-aged man with a job and a home and a family and aches and pains and worries about the future of a country where elections are increasingly purchased like pork bellies and the media meant to alert us to all this are increasingly owned by the corporations doing the purchasing. But when I go fishing, I am merely a human with a fly rod heading off into the woods with a very simple mission: catch a fish. And when I come back from fishing, I come back as a human who has been fishing and, no matter how bad or good the weather or sparse or plentiful the fish, a human who has enjoyed himself without harming other humans or diminishing their fun, a human who has annoyed some fish, it's true, and scared some fish, it's likely, and maybe even killed and eaten some fish, but who has nonetheless been at least briefly alive as a participant in Life and not an uncomprehending observer.

I've been at this too long to learn how to do anything else with my life and thus am stuck with this form of entertainment until it's toes-up time, but if I had it to do over I'd be hard pressed to find a more pleasant way to fritter and waste the hours of the one life I'll ever have, from the huge slices of calendar that disappear beneath cryptic marker scrawlings like "West Branch for Chocolate Caddis" and "Ted and Jim on the Deschutes" to the countless bite-sized chunks that disappear throughout a long dark winter spent hunched over the vise, the wind howling and the trees lashing and the snow encasing the world in frigid silence. And through it all, underpinning it all, with every wrap of hackle or turn of tinsel comes the distant music of rivers, real or imagined—music that's always there, and never stops changing.